THE ACCIDENTAL BLOGGER

On Life – the Good, the
Bad and the Complicated.

Praise for The Accidental Blogger

"Your blogging skills are indeed one of a kind. Captivating, comical, highly informative, witty, inspiring and conversational. Hallmarks of an amazing write. Your tips on life and survival in both territories is nothing short of insightful, and I have no doubt it will serve the same purpose to your readers. Well done."

- Jessie Raymond, book editor.

"Besides the wisdom you shared, I actually love the fact that you use lists. I journal with lists sometimes, because that allows me to get more thoughts down quicker. It really does help in self-thinking and in writing".

- Stuart

"Timely messages… We must indeed move towards a peaceful life".

- Ranti

THE ACCIDENTAL BLOGGER

On Life – the Good, the
Bad and the Complicated.

MICHELLE RONKE

Published in the United Kingdom in 2024 by

Framichi Publications.

www.framichipublications.com

DEDICATION

This book is dedicated to everyone who life may have thrown a few curveballs at, but you swerved and are still standing. Stay strong. Keep on moving!

ACKNOWLEDGEMENT

Without the encouragement and support of my awesome son, my younger brother and some close friends, this book would still be on my list of things to do. Thank you to Alex, Aderanti, Tobi O, Anne and Melissa for helping make this dream come true.

Thank you also to my book publisher, Franca

(Framichi Publications) for that much needed extra push, advice and support. We did it!

PREFACE

◆━━━━━━━━━━●━━━━━━━━━━◆

Becoming a Blogger wasn't a planned journey. I just needed to write my thoughts, as social anxiety had me in a grip of fear. I had become increasingly anxious and isolated during COVID, and it continued after it ended. I'd always been someone who liked to gist about life with close friends and family. As a professional, I also missed sharing opinions with others at work and social networking in a physical setting. I'm sure all of this added to my anxieties.

I thought of writing a book but my anxiety over acceptance held me back. I began to write down my thoughts - it was therapeutic to get things on 'paper' (actually, my iPad). I found it easy to respond to what was happening in my life and the wider world, through my notes, which then became articles for my blogs. I didn't even have to think of what to write; it was already there, in my heart and soul.

So, I wrote and wrote, imbibing experience and logic to the good, not so good and complicated issues. From my experiences of being bi-cultural with a Nigerian British heritage, to writing about what was happening around me or affecting me and everyone else. There were questions asked, relatable advice given - both with a sauce of British humour and Nigerian confidence. What I liked most was just the feeling of achievement in overcoming my daily anxieties and still getting a weekly post out.

I realise that what I was doing was journaling my thoughts. It is a known fact that coherent narrative writing is a recognised therapy for improving mental health. This was my therapy. For that reason, I only promoted my blog with a few friends. But when other bloggers and total strangers also read and left comments, that was a super bonus boost. I have decided to put my blog writings into a book as a witty and motivational read for those that missed my foray into blogging. Will I return. Maybe. I still need my therapy!

Welcome to reflections from my Audacious Life blog. It was written at a time when a lot was happening in my personal life and our world. While preparing this book, I realised that the issues in my blog haven't gone away, and some have intensified. We need to remain audacious and unwavering. I hope it encourages every reader to take a step towards an audacious life too.

TABLE OF CONTENTS

Part One:
LIFE

Chapter 1:

What Do I Know!

Another blogger...! Surely, not what the world needs right now? Well, sorry people, but this woman needs a platform to chat and share valuable lessons about life and our world – the good, the bad and the complicated. It's not a platform to share fake news, troll or debase others. It's a platform for encouraging messages and lessons, influenced not just by my own lived life experiences and knowledge, but also lessons learnt from other people, influences and world happenings. I'm using the talent God gave me – writing; hopefully to impact and encourage others. It's also my therapy for a changed life. Maybe I'll progress to other social media platforms – who knows. But for now, I'm happy right here. So stay with me and let's do some 'amebo' (a Yoruba slang for gossip), and have fun!

I want to write about life, share views about our society, and comment on world situations. You might ask; what qualifies me to do that? Who am I? Depends on how you know me. This could be in my professional or community life, as a friend or a family member. In all, I'm a woman blended in two cultures and languages yet shaped by faith and selected influences (yes, we can all choose who or what influences us). I'm calm, bright and an achiever on the outside but often swirling with anxiety on the inside.

I've lived a life that had a rocky start. Teenage/school girl meets older man and boom, there I was nine months later, just after my mother's 16th birthday. A traumatic relationship that affects my mother till today, and the impact on my childhood is a story for another day, or definitely a book of its own.

Life has smoothed out with age and understanding, but left scars that I'm healing with self-care, daily. There are many stages of my life that I think back on and wish I had the right knowledge and awareness to guide me, at the time. Perhaps I would have made better life decisions. Relationships may have been better, maybe I would have had more children. Maybe I could have had an easier life. Maybe I would have even been dead by now; if life had been too perfect and I didn't learn to fight or struggle for all I've achieved or become today. What do I know.!

I love lists - it's an anxiety tool, so you'll probably get these regularly on my blog. They are not commandments oooo! (The expression oooo! is an African thing - you get it or you don't oooo!). My lists come from my life experiences as well as views or thoughts of other people that I found valuable at certain points of my life. The aim is that it provokes your thoughts too. My first list to you.

FIVE THINGS I DO KNOW ABOUT LIFE:

1. Life can throw curveballs at the best made plans but fear totally crashes it.
2. Time heals if you can forgive, forget and move on.

3. You CAN start again, if you surround yourself with the right people or influences.

4. It's Okay not to be OK. But make sure to take steps or seek help to deal with what's not making you OK. Okay.

5. Self-awareness and self-care is essential to live the life YOU love.

Extra Thought: Be genuinely KIND to others – it is the only act that there is no justified law against… think about it! Trust me on these points. They are golden lessons of life, learnt over the years. I've done the course for you. Use them and be transformed.

- 27th August 2022

Chapter 2:
Audacious Life v Soft Life

Life, from the first breath to the last is unpredictable, but life it is. Whether short or long. Sweet or bitter. Audacious or Soft. Some say life is what we make it. Is it? I've been reading a lot recently about people now craving a soft life. Nobody wants stress or running life on all cylinders. The pandemic has taught us that we CAN slow down. We don't have to be in a physical office to 'work'. It taught us to value life, time, and people. An audacious life is full of energy and boldness. It draws on the survival instinct for success but can sometimes be insensitive to others.

A soft life on the other hand, is more slowly paced, considers comfort and making choices that avoids stress. The Urban Dictionary describes it as the opposite of 'hard life'. It is when you make decisions that leave you feeling stress-free and vibrating higher. It's less about wealth (success) and more about making good choices.

For one who has lived life (and some..!), I think life should be about being audacious, but having a soft life vibe. We need energy and boldness to navigate life but we also need to be kind to ourselves and each other. It can be a difficult balance, but it's what the world needs right now.

- 20th August 2022

Chapter 3:
Life v Likes

One of the newest roles of the past decade which has seemingly eclipsed all other professions but requires no real academic qualifications, is being a social media influencer. It has become one role or lifestyle greatly desired by a certain generation. We have people giving up their careers to become an influencer. Everyone wants to 'break the internet' (such an annoying phrase.). I read a few weeks ago that influencers can and do earn, hundreds of thousands from their status, monthly. Quite a motivation.

As one still dipping my toes into the various platforms of social media, I may be putting myself forward for love or loathing. My close friends know that I practically developed a fear of social media platforms and didn't post much in the last three years. But maybe it was also a needed time for reflection without worrying about who liked me or didn't. Who cared, or who didn't. Who was a Facebook friend or a real friend. It was a time to deal with my anxieties and adverse life experiences. I took them all on with faith, family and friends. Yes, some therapy and counselling too.

So now, I come with more confidence. Not overwhelmed by past mistakes or experiences. I've moved. Maybe that comes with age, experience or maturity. I don't know. But if I have to choose between Likes or Life, I choose Life.

When you choose life, it means you are careful about what you allow to influence your thoughts and emotions. You become more aware of who you are and why self-care is important. You don't withhold good, if it is within your power to do so. You seek to give without expecting anything back. You appreciate life and know that it is a journey, with many starts and stops. And you already know deep down that it will end one day.

As we prepare to bury our dear Queen Elizabeth II, followed by a new era of Kingship with Charles III and a Government led by Liz Truss; let us reflect on what's important for our country and our world.

The last week has given us a time to pause again, as we united to honour our longest reigned monarch. We forgot our rivalry and differences. I pray that this new positive energy will remain and lead to a kinder and fairer society.

With time, we will return to the clamour for 'Likes', as validation of our acceptance by others. Let me leave you with these.

FIVE SOCIAL MEDIA THOUGHTS

1. Go viral or break the internet for the RIGHT reasons

2. See the bigger picture – why is the post/video up. What view is it trying to get you to see or side with.

3. Hundred selfies don't create an identity, only the image the owner wants you to see.

4. Number of followers can go up and go down. It's not a reflection of your true worth (I'm not talking money).

5. Social media can be a force for good with the right writers. You get it...!

- 17th September 2022

Chapter 4:
Best Friend v Bond Friend

I read it recently on Oprah's page that we all are expected to have ten friends in our lives, yet some may even struggle to find five.

But we all need to have friends. Life would be lonely without them – literally. Friends add value and are the fabric we use to cover ourselves. Not all are going to be 'ride or die' friends. Some friends are for a season. Some are acquaintances. Some are for life. I've been blessed with some fantastic friends at each stage of my life. At school. As a single woman. As a mother. As a professional. Some joined my inner circle and remain till today. Life would be so dull without them.

Who do you need in your troupe? I believe you need a good mix of characters to have an Audacious Life and make your world rock. Here's mine.

FIVE TYPES OF FRIENDS TO HAVE (MALE OR FEMALE)

1. **Sassy Friend** - The most lively, vibrant, fun and is definitely glamorous or a fashionista. They drag you to the best hangouts, weddings and parties. The one not to mess with. They give as good as they get. They are battle-ready to defend their friend – cussing or fighting. The one who keeps you moving and connected to the world. They bring more drama than you but you wouldn't have it any other way. Life is never dull or mono.

But you know there is a different side. You know the private person. The one who covers up well on her 'cloudy' days. The one that cooks the most amazing food and invites you round all the time to eat and hear the latest gossip, or watch trending Netflix series. The one who loves being at home just as much as being out.

2. **CCC Friend** - calm, cool, collected. Warns you with sense. Can correct you without being horrible about it. Extremely smart and wise. Probably more educated, knowledgeable and business savvy. Avoids trouble and tries to keep you away from it too. She's your dependable and reliable friend. No last minute cancellations with her, unlike you. You sometimes wonder why they are still your friend with all your 'drama' and *'wahala'* (stress) but you know they are good for you and you for them. They say opposites attracts. You are the 'Yin' to their 'Yang'.

3. **Older Friend** - Someone who is older and matured but is also on your level. They can be formal, fun or unconventional in their approach to life. You can confide in them without worrying about it becoming gossip. Not a relative, but you still give them respect. You dare not call them by their name just like that. As a Nigerian, it's often combined with 'Sis' or 'Brother', sometimes with

a moniker or a subtle nickname. Older friends bring wisdom and share their experiences. If it's an older friend that has really lived a fruitful life, they enrich friendships with shared experiences and lessons, so you can learn from them. They don't want you to make mistakes. They want to see you succeed, even more than them. They mentor and guide. They often know key people and are happy for you to tap into their networks. They can be benevolent and helpful in time of personal or professional challenges.

4. **Prayerful Friend** - The one who doesn't 'joke' with their God or spiritual life. They drag you to their spiritual conferences, men/women meetings or religious celebrations. You must attend oooo! They see you as the 'badass' friend that needs spiritual reawakening but also know you have good values, are kind and helpful to others. They can relate to that part of you. Probably knew each other from way back and they were once as 'badass' as you but got 'saved'. They really have a connection with their God and it shows. We all need to have this ourselves but you know it is not always easy to be consistent or spend enough time on our prayers or spiritual life. I put my hands up. We have times when 'life' distracts. It shouldn't. Prayer warrior type friends won't join you in crazy 'escapades',

they will refuse to attend certain events and will challenge you on moral grounds. But that's okay, you're not offended. Their friendship enriches and keeps you grounded and real. They will always say what is the truth and you can trust their comments or judgements. You also know you can have them as a prayer partner in times of emotional moments.

5. **Bond Friend -** Likely to be someone you've been friends with for a very long time. They are a thread in your life history. Always there at major points. You've shared each other's pains and joys. Your friendship has been tested. Probably had past disagreements and broke up a few times too but always came back as friends – tighter. You can tell this friend pretty much how you're feeling, or how broke/rich you are. Mistakes you made. They get you because they know you. They defend you if others misunderstand you. They are the traditional definition of best friend – not the washed down modern BF version. They have your back. They will post bail for you. They are your 'ride or die'. You only need one. They are very rare. Cherish them.

Which one am I? Which one are you? Do tell.

- 29th October 2022

Chapter 5:
Single Life
v Happy Life

We are still in January, so we can add to our list of what we want for the new year. I was chatting with one of my really good friends (in my circle of five) recently about our single status. Yeah, you read right! We want to change that this year oooo! How? We're still figuring it out but all options are on the table, including online dating websites – reputable ones of course. We're doing our research. 2024 is going to be a leap year, so watch out, I may be the one asking someone, 'will you marry me'. Oh, the thought of me, an African woman, being able to do that. We'll see!

Being Nigerian, female and single at any age past twenty-five, gets you unwanted attention from family and friends. You will continually get asked 'when are you getting married'. Thankfully, I'm at an age where I can say to some of them, *'e fi mi le'* – leave me alone. For younger ones still under thirty – the asking never stops. I'm guilty of doing that too with my younger relatives and Godchildren. It's a passed-on generational trait. We mean no harm oooo!

For now, I'm single and loving life. Is that possible. I don't know, but I'm learning. Personally, I've moved on from clubbing and night party phase but I still enjoy going out with friends or solo. I love fine dining, going to the cinema and travelling. I'm comfortable going to a restaurant and asking 'table for one, please'. Whatever your relationship status, enjoy it.

FIVE WAYS TO LOVE YOUR SINGLE LIFE

1. ***Self-care***: Feeling and looking good. I will always put this at the top of a list for living an Audacious Life, whether single, partnered or married. You know my views. Not repeating here but it really is key.

2. ***Pampering:*** It's easy for life and single life to overshadow our minds and mood, especially when we see others having fun with their partners. But hey, we can enjoy single life, too. Find what works for you and do more of it. My easiest and possibly cheapest mood lifter is getting my nails done. I know many women subscribe to this. You only need to go to a nail salon on a Saturday to confirm. Another thing for me is ensuring I get myself flowers regularly. Nothing extravagant; just nice fresh flowers from the store. Having them in my house makes me feel feminine, warm and special inside. Whenever possible, also plan a spa break - one day is enough. If you can afford longer, why not. Abroad or in a hot climate is even better. You and I can do it. You and I deserve it.

3. ***Travel:*** For me, without a doubt, this is possibly one of the benefits of being single. You can make last minute decisions about travelling. You can take advantage of heavily discounted holiday

packages. You decide where. I love travelling; whether that's for staycation, vacation, or just to wake up in a different room. I'm lucky to be able to do this regularly, solo or with friends. Travelling renews and refreshes. It gets your groove back after all that you have to juggle with daily as a single person. Hey, I've even heard some people found love on their vacations..! Who knows, knows... lol.

4. ***Don't isolate:*** The more places you show up at, the better for your social networks, interactions and even the possibility of meeting someone who ticks your boxes. It can range from social events to learning environments. Paid or free. When last did you attend a conference, speakers' event or exhibition linked to a subject of your interest? There are tons of stuff on Eventbrite. I've made it a point to do as many art or cultural exhibitions as I can. My motto this year is 'show up'. See and be seen. No more excuses.

5. ***Add your own:*** I don't know it all. I need some tips too..!

- 21st January 2023

Chapter 6:

Mental Health v Well-Being

World Mental Health Day comes up on 10 October, and this year's theme is 'making mental health a global priority for all'. Permit me to drill it down to making it a personal priority for all. Why?

Some people view mental health challenges as a sign of weakness. It isn't. Sadly, in some parts of the world, it has been stigmatised to mean a full-blown psychotic episode, or to label someone who doesn't behave 'normal' or to expectations – be it culturally, emotionally or contextually. Whereas, mental health and well-being is part of personal and everyday life. We just call it good days and bad days. It is our well-being (being well), that should become the priority for overcoming mental health challenges.

As we continue this blog life, you'll know more about some of my lived experiences – the good, the bad and the complicated. Before I really became self-aware of who I am and why I do certain things; I was always feeling overwhelmed, constantly exhausted and even feared being rejected or losing friends and relationships. This caused immense havoc with decision making and in my life. I now know that I had undiagnosed Anxiety Disorder, caused by adverse childhood experiences. A high functioning anxiety that often left me feeling alone and close to depression. But I hid it well enough to build my professional career and being the 'rock'; the 'kind' and 'helpful' one, to close friends and family. Until early 2019, when life became unbearable. Then COVID came and made it worse.

In addition to my faith and for the first time, I sought professional help and paid to see a therapist who helped me know the real me. My 'who', and 'why'. He broke it down for me. Thank you, Jakub. That started my journey from mental health to mental well-being. It's why I can talk openly. It's why I want to share, for others to learn and live an Audacious Life. I'm not a therapist but this is my therapy; writing. I'm more empowered but still on my journey. I'm now more aware of how to respond to my anxieties and 'moments'.

My message for Mental Health Day is to not let anxiety, depression or any mental health challenge, clip your wings or stop you from reaching your goals. Take your mental well-being awareness and journey, one step at a time. Trust me, life does get better.

Big up to church Pastors, who are removing the negative beliefs around faith and mental health. Pastor Keion Henderson of Lighthouse Church Texas and the awesome Sarah Jakes Roberts of One Church, we feel your impact and influence.

FIVE BABY STEPS TO MENTAL WELL-BEING

1. Don't be afraid of being labelled. There is more understanding and support for people affected by mental health.

2. Learn more about your 'condition'. Get it diagnosed professionally if you need to. Understand the

'what', 'why' and 'how', in order to manage it or recover properly.

3. Accept your vulnerability and seek the type of help and support you are comfortable with. There are many options; medical, therapeutic, spiritual, nutritional, cognitive, and the list goes on.

4. Be more self-aware. Know your 'triggers' and have a coping mechanism for that moment. Listening to sounds or using a breathing or relaxation technique is recommended.

5. Self-care is critical. Do more of what makes you happy or relaxed, but doesn't cause damage or new addictions. From simple things like having your nails done, fine dining, going to the cinema, to taking short travel breaks. Just do it.

- 8th October 2022

Chapter 7:

Mother v Mothering

HAPPY MOTHERING DAY

March has indeed been a month for acknowledging us women. Early this month we celebrated International Women's Day. Tomorrow will be Mother's Day in the UK.

Our world is changing with issues surrounding gendering. Someone born as a female can no longer claim exclusive rights to be a woman. The same applies to men. This is our new world of gender and gendering. I'm still forming a view.

In our new world, soon any self-defined gender will be able to have a child and become a mother. Mother and mothering are intertwined, but definitely mean different things. Let me explain.

I visited an art gallery last week to view an exhibition of British Impressionist painters of the 19th and 20th century when there was a move away from the focus by artist on medieval mythology, to more reflections on the interplay between working people, families at leisure and the landscapes they lived in. Everyday life reflected through vivid colours and impressions. One particular painting, The Breadwinners (Newlyn Fishwives), by Walter Langley (1852-1922), caught my eye. It depicted some women/mothers in the 19th century from a Cornish coastal village in the UK, walking along the seashore while carrying heavy baskets of fish brought in by fishermen that day. Fish destined for market. No animal or vehicle to help the women carry it there. The loads were solidly on their backs. Why they call us the weaker sex, I'll never fully understand. It made me reflect on the wonder that a woman is, always has been, and will continue to be.

While fishing and farming conditions have improved in the UK, many women in poorer nations still use what they have, to ensure they can feed their families. From those who plant yams and cassava on their farms with crude back breaking instruments of hoes and cutlasses, to women who provide services to carry heavy shopping on their heads in the local markets or move large goods around for traders. Yes, men do it too, but not necessarily to feed their family. Think about it. From my experience, when you see a woman doing hard manual labour like her life depends on it – there is a child or children on her mind. A child that needs to be fed or has essential school costs to be met. That's the difference between Mother and Mothering.

So, it was disheartening to read about a daughter that took her eighty-two-year-old mother to court in London, to evict her mother from a property that she has lived in for over forty years. Worked two shifts a day as a nurse to pay for it. Ownership title had been transferred years before to the daughter, to avoid UK inheritance tax. As the daughter is in her early fifties, I can assume she also grew up in the same property as a child. I'm not judging or claim to know the full facts of the case, but there are some situations that need to be avoided or walked away from.

I am not stating that all Mothers are treasures. They are not. Trust me on this. Thankfully those who fail in their duty of mothering, are in the minority.

Whatever type of mother you have or had – good, bad or complicated, be kind and remember her on Mothering Sunday. Even if it's only in your heart. I'm preaching to myself here. God help me, you, and all of us with complicated mother and child relationships.

Happy Mother's Day to all Mothering women who put their children's needs before their own. Mothers who sold their precious gold jewellery or expensive fabrics to send children to university. Who went hungry or drank 'garri' with water because the cooked food wouldn't go round. Who had to give 'IT' up for survival. Mothers who worked tirelessly to ensure their children were kept safe, fed daily, went to school and had a happy childhood relative to their family circumstances and local community. We celebrate you. May you enjoy the fruits and joys of your labours.

- 18th March 2023

Chapter 8:

Kindness v Thoughtfulness

SHOWING REAL KINDNESS

Kindness and service has been used a lot recently by both the mighty and not so. We need to put it in perspective and add thoughtfulness to our actions if we truly wish to see the effect of kindness. Let me explain.

A few weeks ago, a friend of mine received and shared a video of a young Nigerian man, found wandering on the streets of a town in America. He was stopped, questioned and filmed by another Nigerian man in a car. The man asked the young guy some questions. It was obvious from the exchange that the young man was disorientated or having an 'episode'. The man continued to film and question him about what he was doing walking the streets and which part of Nigeria he was from. I found the video quite disturbing. I guess the person filming had good intentions - perhaps out of concern or to help locate the young man's family. However, he was sharing a video of a vulnerable person in a state of distress and disorientation. Many others have done the same, or similar. This is kindness without thoughtfulness.

How to show real kindness? The most amazing act of service or kindness are often the ones not seen. Done away from the cameras or not posted online. If it is; it should be with thoughtfulness and consideration for the recipient of that kindness. Filming someone in distress or in their time of difficulty is sometimes not always the best way to get a message across, or appeal to the compassion of others. Use the appropriate image. After all, they say the internet never forgets. Why keep a reminder of a difficult phase of someone's life forever online. We can use words to describe or appeal for help – people still read.

Nowadays, I don't often agree with Megan Markle on what she has to say, but I concur with comments made during her speech at a recent awards ceremony in New York (yes, THAT one linked to the 'near catastrophic' car chase involving paparazzi!). While accepting her award she said, 'you can charter a path in which you repeat daily; in your daily acts of service, in kindness, advocacy, in grace and fairness'. Let me help out in giving this context.

I'm a Rotarian. We are guided by what we call the Four-Way Test of what we say, think and do. Whether a Rotarian or not, if we ALL applied these principles or similar, we may just be able to make our world beautiful again. I dearly hope so.

THE ROTARY FOUR-WAY TEST

- Is it the TRUTH?

- Is it FAIR to all concerned?

- Will it build GOODWILL and BETTER FRIENDSHIPS?

- Will it be BENEFICIAL to all concerned?

LAST WORD

Incidentally last week was Mental Health Awareness Week in the UK. Even more reason to apply the four-Way test to each other. If nothing else, Be Kind. Be thoughtful.

- 20th May 2023

Chapter 9:
Adversity v Hope

AUDACIOUS HOPE OVERCOMES

I've been back at uni this week for face-to-face lectures. My course focusses on understanding and responding to one of one of life's most brutal and sometimes fatal incidents; domestic violence, which happens to both male and female. The Crime Survey for England and Wales (CSEW) estimated 2.4 million adults aged 16 years and over experienced domestic abuse in the year ending March 2022. This is a prevalence rate of approximately 5 in 100 adults. I can go on with the statistics but not today. I just need you to understand the prevalence of what is still very much an under-reported crime in Black communities – particularly African and new migrant communities in the UK. Very worrying.

Why have I chosen to put myself through another post-graduate study when I could be chilling. I ask myself oooo. When you've been though life, (I've had a complex one but no longer a victim of it), you want to know more about the 'why', 'what' and 'how' in order to overcome difficulties or adversity. You want to make a difference and help others when it happens to them. Adversity or negative life events comes to all of us at different times or with levels of severity. One thing that has been proved through endless research is that our life experiences shape our disposition, traits, character, habits and resilience.

Divorce/separation, bereavement, job/financial losses, poor-health/terminal illness are often referred to as some of the main life events that impact the course of a person's life. And there are many more. Who experiences it, knows it.

What I've learnt about adversity or challenging life events, is hope. Audacious Hope is what gives birth to Audacious Life. The two go together. The Bible guides us that Hope is to trust in God's assurances and faith is the promise that if one acts now, the requests that will come from hope will be fulfilled in the future. Hope and faith are intertwined, and each is necessary for exaltation.

I love going to the cinema, alone or with a friend. It's the only way I can watch a film without being distracted by email, text, calls or worry. Unusual for me, but I watched a film to the end on my iPad last night in the hotel that I stay when in Worcester for uni. The film is titled 'Enoch' and is a biofilm about the life of Enoch Adeboye, the head of the Redeemed Christian Church - please Google. I've only ever known him in his current role and had no real back story. The film helped fill in the gaps and I totally recommend it. That such a great man came from such abject poverty and was able to excel despite all obstacles is another remarkable life.

The story of Enoch Adeboye, from very poor beginnings, to one of the greatest influencers of his generation, is a testimony to the Audacity of Hope. My life experiences, yours and countless others who have overcome whatever life has thrown and are still standing, is evidence of Hope.

There are many situations going on in the world today – some reported in news headlines; Ukraine War, earthquakes in Turkey, migrants risking their lives to cross oceans to safer countries, etc. Some are not in the news, but we hear about personal tragedies of friends and families. How do I console a friend who suddenly lost her husband at age fifty eight, with no prior illness – healthy in the morning, dead in the afternoon. How do I support an uncle recently diagnosed with HIV. How do I encourage a nephew who lost his job and has a young family to still provide for. I and others with similar situations, can only try with Audacious Hope. I'm off to Worcester Cathedral now for some uplifting and hope renewal.

- 11th March 2023

Chapter 10:

A Changed Life

LIFE AFTER COVID

What a week I've had. Hence, this is coming out a day late to my usual schedule – thanks to those who texted me to check. Really wish I could share, here, but don't feel ready. Hopefully, soon enough, some lessons will come out of it that I can share. We have to keep striving for an Audacious and happy life, no matter what life throws at us. We keep moving.

I've been reflecting a lot recently on how our life and world has changed after COVID. Some good, some not as much. Some for ever.

COVID introduced us to a new way of life that was supposed to be temporary. Lockdown and isolation. Mask wearing. Social distancing. Working from home. Virtual meetings and celebrations. We all embraced it. Did we have a choice?

I still remember attending my first Zoom wedding and funeral service. Who would have thought that would be the norm in our world. I currently have so many invitations for virtual events and meetings that when I see an invite for a physical event, I'm so delighted. Don't get me wrong, I like virtual events too. It has opened up new connections with friends and associates. I've joined professional forums in America and Africa, and it's been amazing to learn and share good practice. It's also enabled me and other school friends who live in the UK to take part in our

Nigerian secondary school alumni monthly meetings. It's renewed and strengthened friendships. Can you believe that this June, we'll be celebrating our 40th anniversary of leaving secondary school? Yes, I'm showing my age oooo!... but where do you think the experiences and lessons come from. Lol.

COVID has shown us that when it comes to it, change is possible. We can do things differently. We can break the norm and habits of a lifetime.

While we have suspended a lot of COVID measures – some only very recently, we still need to be prepared to change old ways and even some new ones.

COVID connected the world much more with social media and information. It also, in my view, created a 'wokeness' built on anger and an 'only me' culture. Some people feel invisible behind their screens and have become warriors without a legitimate cause. Life is measured by reviews, likes and comments.

Our world is heading to a dangerous point where reality becomes the 'fake news' because nobody knows what is real again. This is the change most feared. We only need to read comments, views, and opinions presented by so called 'influencers'. To have millions of 'followers' on social media is great, but what followers fail to realise is that most 'influencers' have paymasters – whether that is advertisers, organisations or individuals. This is my main concern with our changed world.

Who or what we allow to influence us is the deal breaker for our future. Wars will be started or lost by this. Politicians will be elected or deselected on this. Hate will be built on this. Humanity will be less kind by this. Think about it. Because I am.

As I watch what is being posted online or shared via WhatsApp about the coming general elections in Nigeria, my country of heritage, I worry oooo. I pray for a peaceful election. I pray for a peaceful world. I pray for the end of wars in our world.

MY FIVE PENNIES, KOBO OR CENTS FOR INFLUENCERS AND ONLINE COMMENTATORS.

1. Be kind with your views and comments. Or don't comment at all, if it's not needed or will not bring positive change.

2. Are your views, comments valid? If not, why post. Why chase clout.

3. Have you fact-checked your sources before you post? It's easily done.

4. If you've had a negative experience, avoid toxic responses as it will dilute the message or feedback intended to give. Our comments should be with

a view to enable improvements; not to cause deliberate damage or social tensions.

5. You're not invisible. One day you may meet the person you have insulted or written about. Will you still be able to repeat what you wrote?

- 19th February 2023

Chapter 11:

Family Life – It's Complicated

Wow, someone who I won't name has been busy washing their princely laundry this year - and we're still in January. How did things get this way. The Spare has gone spare (British, informal. : to become very angry or upset). Whatever your views about the now infamous 'Spare', please don't judge quickly. Some of us know how he feels. Rejection is a terrible feeling and can skew the mind and warp reality. As the palace said, 'recollections may vary'. It's funny how we think riches and privilege bring happiness or make us immune to emotional pain, but it doesn't.

I guess, (actually, I know) we all have our own family issues, some that are so deep and complicated. I've referred to my own family background briefly, but it's more complicated and emotionally challenging than I can share. Think of an issue, and I can definitely show you aspects of it in my family relationship history. Some things are too dark. I'm not even going there. But I'm not alone. I know many friends with similar family relationship experiences. Some are estranged, while some carry on and live with the emotional pain. Some survive and flourish, despite it all (like I chose to do). Some don't and live a depressed and unhappy life, longing for what will never happen (like I used to do).

On the flip side, I know so many families that have seemingly happy relationships with each other. They also have issues but don't allow their differences to fester and disrupt. They look out for each other – you fight one, you fight all. They support and lift each other – they are not 'crabby' and pulling each other down. I know this because I experienced it with my childhood foster family (yes, I was privately fostered, as was common with African families in the sixties and seventies) and now have same love from my adopted or chosen families. If you're in such a family unit, cherish it. I seriously envy you.

I'm not a family relationship expert, but do I have personal experience of complex family dramas – believe me, I do. Here are my tips to surviving it!

FIVE TIPS AND LESSONS TO SURVIVE FAMILY DRAMAS.

1. Silence can be golden. Hold your 'truth'. It doesn't make you weak, it strengthens and unites when you forgive or forget – ideally both. A Nigerian proverb, loosely translated says 'words are like eggs, once broken cannot be repaired'. It may also not leave room for future reconciliation. Words can go deep and if it's in our power, it's best to say nothing rather than cut others with our words. If you must speak your truth (and talking therapy is good, despite some views), then do so with someone who is able to listen and guide.

2. Remove yourself if you have to, temporarily or more long term. I know not everyone can do

this, especially while still a child. But as we reach adulthood and become more independent; it may be the best option. If you have tried all that is in your ability to talk, challenge or ignore what causes you hurt from your family and there's no real meeting point or willingness to work things through mutually and with respect; then make your move. It may be a slow withdrawal or reduced engagement. But not driven by malice or anger. Leave space for tomorrow and reconciliation. At the least leave contact info available or keep connected with a family member you can still relate to. You're still a family member and you never know, they may need to call you for good or sad news.

3. Don't lash out or blame yourself. It is easy to do so, but it only damages you even more. We can't choose our biological families but we are unique from each other, irrespective of shared DNAs, heritage, or upbringing. You can evolve beyond the background you were born into – whether that is poor or rich, loved or neglected. These things can shape your thinking, but they don't limit you. I'm an advocate for self-care and awareness of WHO you are. That has less to do with the family background you come from.

4. Embed yourself in a 'new' family that gives you a good perspective of what a loving family can be like. These can be extended family or friends. They can buffer you from the issues at home, show you kindness and care about you like their own children. They encourage you to be the best you can. Over time, you become an accepted member of the family. Your own family 'ishes', will soon begin to have less impact on you or your world. Trust me, it worked for me.

5. Have a good friend that you can share your experience with. A friend you trust won't share your story as gossip or for clout.

May we all find healing from whatever troubles us. I'll say Amen to that!

- 14th January 2023

Chapter 12:

Thankful Life

Celebrated another birthday yesterday. For me, the past year has been anything but ordinary. Why? I 'got my groove back' and became more determined to be the person, I used to be. Living an Audacious Life. Not one wracked daily by anxiety, as I have been in the last few years. This new energy got me to start my blog, begin a new study course and write a book (coming soon). I have a lot to be thankful for.

Again, as my birthdays have become, it was a time for a short break for reflections. I chose to spend a few days in Brussels. I'm still here as I write. Usually, I like to go somewhere hot, since November is always cold in Britain. But I couldn't face the hassle of airline and airport shenanigans, post pandemic. Who wants to wait hours for immigration checks or to book a flight at the risk of cancellation. I will only fly now if it's absolutely unavoidable – or at least until airport issues improve.

So this year, I travelled by Eurostar. I haven't used this mode of travel for a while but what a pleasant re-discovery. Not having to worry about packing liquids. Even, not worrying about the weight of my luggage. Travel bliss.

Brussels has been fabulous. Very friendly people (better than one other European country I won't mention but the clue is it starts with letter F).

Brussels is an old city, so lots of lovely churches, museums and buildings to see. Not that I've done much of that on this trip oooo, as my hotel was just awesome and offered so much inside.

One thing I did discover about Brussels is how they have different ethnic neighbourhoods, and each is unique and feels like you are in the country or continent of its origin. The 'African mall' is just like back 'home'. The 'Moroccan' area at Garde Norde, is like I walked into a Marrakesh market or Istanbul neighbourhood. They co-exist with the wider areas of the city and community, and they are not isolated to inner ghettos. This brings about great community cohesion. Not heard much of ethnic riots in Belgium, have you.

Anyway, enough of my social commentary. I had a fun time in Brussels with one of my oldest and best friend. Just the two of us being girls again. Shopping, eating healthy food (she is a health coach, so I have no choice). One crazy thing we did was the famous Brussels Pub Crawl. What happened in Brussels will stay in Brussels, but I can say it was probably one if the best birthday night outs I've had recently. Salut!

FIVE THINGS TO BE THANKFUL FOR EVERY DAY.

1. For waking up to a new day and another chance to achieve your life goals - even if it's the ones you've set for that day alone. One day at a time.

2. For freedom of mind and choice. Even with a

restricted environment or limited capacity, you can choose how it affects you.

3. For hope in the midst of turmoil or anxiety. Knowing that a new day has come to bring you closer to what you hope for but have not yet received. Our faith tells us to wait patiently with diligence and working with purpose.

4. For every thoughtful word, message, or kindness shown to you by others. Thankful that you can also do the same for others.

5. For not giving up. Still moving. I know that not everyone gets to be thankful for all of these essential elements of life but if you can count at least three of them a day, say thank you.

- 5th November 2022

Chapter 13:
What's Going On – Hard Life?

It's usually said that the 'Ember months' – September to December, often bring many challenges, as the year closes. In Nigeria, the fear of the 'ember months' is the beginning of wisdom. We are told to be extra careful, particularly when travelling. I'm not sure what statistics support these travel apprehensions, but I think it's because there are usually more people going to their respective towns for Christmas and New Year celebrations. With the state of our roads and general security issues, I'd advise caution anytime of the year. But this rant is not about my still much-loved Nigeria.

As we face another winter in the UK, it is palpable with discontent. I have to ask what's going on in Britain right now. Train strikes, more strikes, eco-zealots causing mayhem, cost of living crises, budget fears, illegal immigration and asylum tensions, fears of war. Constant rain and storms – in winter!

I'm usually a resilient-minded person and I just 'soldier' on with everything life throws at me – I've had a lot, believe me but I'm still here. This month and even the last week has been tougher than usual. Coming back after my short European city break last week, I arrived to meet a closed station that would have given me a thirty minute journey home. Instead, I had to reroute to a journey of nearly two hours, in pouring rain and with luggage (darn all that shopping for fabrics!). I really should have taken a cab but I went into panic mode, and I was not thinking straight initially.

Same with my journey to university this week. I've had to deal with my pre-booked train being cancelled due to strike action and I'm not even sure about how I will get back home from Worcester, today. I won't talk about my disrupted journey on the M25, earlier this week, or how my smart meter is telling me my heating bill this month is likely to be higher than my monthly mortgage payments – I joke you not.

We can only take so much. But the signs are that there's still more to come. God help us.

How are you coping? My advice is limited but these may help.

FIVE TIPS TO SURVIVING ECONOMIC HARD TIMES

1. Please look on your council website for information about help available locally in your area.

2. Look at recognised consumer websites about ways to reduce your heating costs with small lifestyle adjustments.

3. Look at pooling together with family or friends to bulk-buy food and household items. This can significantly reduce your shopping bills.

4. Even if you have always worked and never had to ask for assistance before, don't hesitate or let 'pride' prevent you from taking up offered help.

It could be donations, help with food items, discounts, and government payments. Please find out what's available. It should not be a 'heat or eat' situation, even in these challenging times.

5. If you're struggling financially, particularly with your rent or mortgage payments, please check your eligibility for state benefits/assistance and make a claim. We are a welfare state for such time as this. We take care of those in need, whether temporarily or long term. We've paid for it – you and me. Now is the time to use it.

Please look out for each other at this time. Be Kind. Everyone is finding it hard – rich and poor. Ask Elon Musk and Mark Zuckerberg.

- 12th November 2022

Chapter 14:

Decluttered Life

DEFINE YOUR SPACE

In this life, we need to declutter frequently, or we end up carrying unnecessary baggage or becoming labelled as a hoarder. I am terrible at getting rid of things. My son gets exasperated with what I'm still holding on to for 'just in case'. We've had many arguments when he's cleared out my kitchen cupboards and my plastic souvenirs – the ones usually given at Naija parties that you don't actually use. I also love a bargain – whether I need it or not. Right now, my house is just so cluttered that I'm very worried about being labelled a hoarder in my old age. I envy people who keep a minimalistic home environment – definitely a future goal for me.

I remember clearing out my father's home after he passed away. What a shock that was. He had items he'd kept from the seventies. So many documents that were out of date or personal items that had no relevance to his life at the age he died. We even saw our old school report cards. My older brother's reports were hilarious, and despite all the negative comments from his secondary teachers, he's turned out to be one of my most successful siblings. I'm immensely proud of how he turned his life around. Well done Dapo – Black Diamond.

It's good to keep SOME things for memories or if we may need later. I discovered more about my father after his death; from going through his documents, photos, notes, and letters that he had kept. Thanks to my father, I was also able to find some of my early childhood photos, documents and mementoes. I cherish these so much, and they filled in many gaps about his life and mine too. Miss you Pops.

I read a strange expression recently that said 'If the sun is too hot on your skin – take it down'. Hmmm, how do you do that. I might not be able to physically take the sun down, but I can sure take some things that are not good for me, out of my life.

So, in preparation for a year of calm and purpose, I've started decluttering. Starting with my phone contact list, there will be calls I will no longer pick. Not for malice but to keep me focussed on what and who is really important in my life right now. If you only call when you need something from me, or send only forwarded texts, or if you sap my energy and increase my anxiety, then you have been DECLUTTERED! I'm happy to be decluttered too as it's a two-way street. No beef. No *wahala*.

FIVE THINGS TO DECLUTTER FOR
A NEW YEAR OR BEGINNING

1. Mind. Declutter it of all pain and betrayal of the past. Don't let it make you lose focus on YOU.

2. Work. It must balance with life. Not taking on more than we need at the stage of life we are. The young

can run and not go weary. But it's not like that as you get older. If we have to step down from some official positions or professional activities – then do that.

3. Friends. As we grow older our circle needs to be smaller and meaningful. Tough decisions may have to be made. Who do you really need or want as a friend? You decide.

4. Physical environment. I've already mentioned about keeping things we don't need, but it's also important to not even buy them in the first place – bargain or not.

5. Future plans. We sometimes overdo what we want to do. It's wise to be realistic about our capacity and ability to meet personal goals, resolutions, or visions. We all need a plan for our life but this should be regularly reviewed and refreshed. It makes it meaningful and achievable. It leads to an Audacious Life.

Have a wonderful and Audacious year ahead.

- 7th January 2023

Chapter 15:

Back To School
– New Life

Wasn't sure how to title this but I really wanted to share my past week's experience. Yes, I went back to school, (okay, okay, university!), to study for another postgraduate degree qualification that I hope will give me 'locus standi' or authority to talk about a social issue close to my heart. After nearly twenty years since my last academic study. What a shock I've had.

Don't get me wrong. Over the years, I have completed numerous training courses for skills acquisition, professional accreditation and personal development but this is different. The last time I was in university, blackboards/whiteboards were solidly installed on lecture room walls. Lecturers got their fingers blotted with those often squeaky, leaky coloured marker pens. Printed notes and hand-outs were given out during lectures. Woe betide, if you weren't in class to collect yours and then have to beg friends who attended, to let you copy theirs. Books were taken out from the library – if they weren't already loaned to other students, as was the case most of the time. God help you if you failed to return a borrowed book – you didn't get your degree certificate issued, if you didn't pay the necessary fines (my own experience but I paid it oooo! lol).

Now, it's all about going online. You apply, register, pay fees, read books/articles, have class discussions, and submit assignments. All online. Lecturers post their notes and presentations on the online blackboard. Virtual lectures are posted online for you to access and undertake course activities within a limited time period, or it's considered a 'missed class'. Don't even think of plagiarising because specialist softwares will find you out in a jiffy.

When we have had physical lectures on campus, technology followed. White screens and overhead projectors – no fussy coloured markers. Students come primed with their personal laptops/iPads to take notes, with very few pens in sight. I've stuck to writing my notes on paper, but for how long before I leave my 'old school' ways.

I'm not complaining. I'm loving every day of my return to university (or Uni, as everyone has abbreviated it to). I welcome this new experience to gain further insights into social theories and develop a stronger critique approach to the generation of new ideas and solutions for society problems. I will share more on my uni experience again. For me, at the end of the day, it's about learning life – or is that lifelong learning. Wish me luck!

FINAL THOUGHT!

As Confucius stated, "learning without reflection is a waste. Reflection without learning is dangerous". Permit me to paraphrase this to 'Living without learning is a waste. Living without development is dangerous'.

- 24th September 2022

Chapter 16:

What's Love Got To Do With It?

say plenty. A popular song from the 80s, asks that question; because a heart can be broken. I wrote recently about single life and hopefully finding love. I'm still on it. Wish me luck.

What is love? While we often relate love with intimacy, it's sizeably more than that and I would even say it's what happens after or beyond that. Sometimes it is totally and evidently absent in what should be an intimate experience.

Who has not been shocked by the recent arrests and trials of sexual predators and offenders. We've read about this so much recently with the alarming revelations about behaviours of men towards women - especially those who had a duty to protect women, as police officers.

Even more worrying, children being violent towards children; seen recently in the violent attack of a young schoolgirl by other young girls - the race factor is worrying but to me, it is secondary. Why. The level of hate and violence shown by those young children towards another is a sign of the society we are creating.

I was also at uni a few weeks ago for lectures. My course which focuses on understanding intimate partner violence has really made me reflect on what we call 'love', and why it can quickly switch to hate and violence. It's not easy learning about this subject but it has been a revelation of understanding the dynamics of the heart and mind. Sometimes it has been very triggering, when

I remember my own past relationship experiences. I will persevere and see this course through, so I can inform and support others better.

Valentine's Day is a few days away and love will be celebrated around the world. Like Christmas, some will go over the top. Some will fake it but it's worth remembering what love is. I'm not going to claim to be wiser than the creator of the universe, so I will borrow from Holy Scriptures which should guide you; whatever your spiritual or religious beliefs may be.

FIVE THINGS LOVE IS

1. Patient

2. Kind

3. Does not envy or boast

4. Is not arrogant or rude

5. Does not insist on its own way

Love yourself first, is rule 101 for an Audacious Life. I hope you enjoy Valentine's Day and can truly celebrate love with or without someone beside you. May love be true for you. May love be real for you. Whatever your plans for Valentine's Day, enjoy.

- 11th February 2023

Chapter 17:
Heat Or Chill

For those of us living in the UK, winter can be very cold. This year has been brutally harsh – not just in respect of the minus zero temperatures, but the cost of keeping warm. I jokingly wrote previously that my smart meter was showing that my bill for that month was going to be more than my mortgage. It came to pass this month. I got the email billing yesterday. I'm still trying to understand how I used so much electricity and gas despite all my efforts to cut down. I tire ooo/fed up. Working from home is becoming more expensive than it's worth. Savings made on transport costs and lunch is being erased with the increasing cost of keeping warm while you work.

I don't know how families on lower incomes are coping. This worry over heating bills and every other bill has become the topic of discussion for most of us. I know that I try to make light of things that seem unreal but what we joke about today seems to come true later. Many of my friends are so concerned about keeping elderly parents warm and the significant cost coming along with it; that they are already planning to move parents temporally to Nigeria if the cold weather continues. At least they will be warm, and it will be more affordable than the cost of heating their parents' home in the UK. I'm sure even non-Naijas will start thinking of moving elderly family members to warmer climates during winter. It will be cheaper. Gosh, I see a whole new industry here. I don't want to digress.

Cost of living crisis is real - for everyone. I'm not surprised we have strikes everywhere and possibly more to come - Job Centre staff just announced theirs. We feel their anger of working and not being able to meet the basic cost of living. I think it's totally unacceptable that nurses and other key workers have to resort to food banks to eat or feed their families. Some of our politicians really do need to experience the real world and leave their cosseted Parliament capsules. Did one of them recently say that people should budget better. Statements like that caused the French revolution and got Maria Antoinette her place in history.

How did we get here? I don't know. So many reasons being given - Russia, gas supply, Ukraine war, etc. Whatever it is please, please, can someone sort this out. Next winter might just find me on those picket lines, protesting.

Of course, this wasn't my intended focus for today as I had something much more important to talk about, but THAT bill just floored me! Hope yours was not as shocking and if it was, don't let it stress you. Keep warm and the heating bill will work itself out in due course. Roll on summer.!

- 28th January 2023

Chapter 18:

April: A Month Of Awe

HAPPY NEW MONTH

Goodness me, we're already in the fourth month of the year. April 1st or April Fool's Day in some countries. I'm not pranking, though I've fallen for some pretty good ones. What's yours? Do share.

A new month is always filled with great expectations. Just like New Year, we now get monthly greetings in our online message boxes, wishing us Happy New Month. I've spent half the morning trying to respond to mine. I think it's rude not to reply to good wishes. A new month for me, is like a reminder that I still have a lot to do before the end of the year. Goals to meet and commitments to prepare for. It's a time to reflect on the last month and check what's in my diary for the new month – weddings, birthdays, study trips, holidays, blogging, writings, etc. This is without knowing what issues the 'day job', will bring and how I must continually focus on my well-being and self-care.

April is already looking packed. I've got a wedding and I'm off again to 'you know where'. I'll also be spending Easter holidays there. I'm still struggling with packing – that's another stress. But I'm so excited to be getting away from the cold and rain we're getting in the UK at the moment.

April is also the start of the financial year for most businesses. It generally means new price increases for everything. One British newspaper has described this month as Awful April; as Council tax, water, broadband and mobile phone bills go up this month.

Incredibly, this April is also a Holy Month for many religions as we celebrate Easter, Passover and the end of Ramadan. Whichever faith you adhere to, may your prayers be answered. May you be freshly blessed. May divine peace keep our world safe.

Happy New Month. Happy celebrations and festivals.

- 1st April 2023

Chapter 19:
New Additions

TRY NEW EXPERIENCES

Life has been hectic lately – a period of emotional ups and downs. Also a bit overwhelming with work and assignment deadlines (who send me oooo!), so I've been looking forward to this bank holiday weekend. It will give me time to spend with the new 'family' addition.

I must share. Just got a 'fur grand-baby'. Ye gods, I never imagined I'd ever write such words. But life surprises us. My son and his girlfriend just bought a puppy together – a toy poodle. He's about ten weeks old. Before getting the poodle, they had asked for my views about him being in my home sometimes. What sort of talk is that. I vehemently said 'noooo'. Can you imagine. These millennial people - don't they know most Africans generally don't like cats and dogs in the house. We have enough *wahala* or stress in our life. Anyway, they still got the pet. I was the first person they brought him to see and handed him to me like a new baby. I couldn't help it. I fell in love instantly with the bundle of fur, chocolate button nose and cute brown eyes that stared up at me. They named him Mocha - to reflect the coffee and chocolate colour of his fur.

Let me tell you, I get it now, why some people don't joke with their pets. Mocha is adorable and easy to love. He has abundant energy and demands as much attention as any toddler that is just discovering a new environment. I had the task of 'Nana duties' last weekend. By the second day, I was exhausted, but loving this new experience. I pray this is practice for when the real grand kids come. Amen.

How does all this connect with an Audacious Life attitude. Well, it's about trying new things. Overcoming our negative past experiences. Being ready to love someone or something again. Mocha has reset my emotions about having a pet. He has shown me the challenges of getting them housetrained – the number of times we have to go out for a wee is exhausting. But it has also shown the love that you get back when you are kind. I remember when Mocha saw me again after I returned from Nigeria last week – he yapped and jumped, with so much excitement. That 'choke'. Even my big sis, who doesn't like dogs much has been won over by Mocha. That's saying something.

In the coming wonderful month of May, we not only have three bank holidays (an additional extra), but also new additions to governance and headship in the two countries that I call home. Next week in the UK, is the official coronation of King Charles III. At the end of May will be the swearing in of our own 'Jagaban' and incoming President of Nigeria, Bola Tinubu. Whether we loath or love them as individuals, they will influence many aspects of our life in the coming years. And we shall all be watching.

Have a great May Day Bank Holiday

- 30th April 2023

Chapter 20:
Black History Month

October is generally Black History Month. I understand the relevance but struggle to get it. Why just a month, when we need awareness every day and to celebrate our Black heroes more openly.

I love history, or seeing things from the past. My favourite scholars, philosophers, theologians and artists are referenced in history and critical world periods. I enjoy visiting ancient buildings and heritage sites. I sometimes think I must have lived before because I get goosebumps walking through a building full of history. Nothing makes me more mindful of how far mankind has come in knowledge and innovation than when I see buildings that have been here for hundreds and even thousands of years. Only a 'soulless' person will not have the inexplainable feeling of enthralment or spiritual reflection.

I also enjoyed history as a subject at school. The history and traditions of the Tudors and Victorians fascinated me, still does. Who can forget the six wives of King Henry VIII, who we remember as divorced, beheaded, died, divorced, beheaded, survived. However, I have no memory of being educated about my heritage as a Black schoolchild in seventies England. I do however, hear that things are different now in schools. Thank goodness.

I feel that I was let down. I had a right to know about Black history and the heroes that made a difference to our world. To know that black people have been in the UK for centuries and have been an integral part of its development. I had a right to know about the great heroes of the African continent, not just that the main habitation always had a thatched roof or that all Black people lived in extreme poverty or in jungle settings with wild animals. That's what I was told, and the images I saw in my reading books. That's what I believed. Until my mother took me back home to live in Nigeria when I was fifteen. I saw the true beauty of Africa and our amazing homes. I heard of the rich Black history that came through school lessons about the beauty of the Benin Empire, the battles of Northern Caliphates, and of course my Oduduwa heritage. I fell in love with Africa and found my Black pride. Have never lost it. Never will.

Today, in the UK, we stand on the cusp of probably electing our first non-white Prime Minister. They say the Conservative Party is fighting for its soul. Really? I see it more than that. For a country that Black people of all hues, have contributed to and sacrificed their lives for in war and peace; it's time for the next level of 'First'. We will know in a few days.

I think it's ironic that it's the Conservatives - (a party traditionally made up of rich white males, some probably with family history linked to slavery), are the ones presenting the UK with the most credible opportunity for an ethnic minority to lead their party and be Prime Minister. They also gave us the first female Prime Minster in the UK and we've had two more, since Thatcher. What's up Labour, or as we say in Nigeria, 'Labour, how far now'. Sorry, I try to keep off political views but hey, couldn't resist that one.

FIVE THINGS TO REMEMBER
AS A PERSON OF COLOUR;

1. Your colour is non-negotiable and your history isn't either.

2. Don't just be taught your history; seek it for yourself. Put a visit to Africa or your country of heritage, in your bucket list. Experiencing or seeing it is better than reading or hearing about it.

3. Black lives really do matter – not in the BLM way but in knowing that you have the same value as anyone else.

4. The mind is the greatest prison, if we don't open it to what is the truth. Have your own views about who you are as a Black person. You can be different. We don't need herd mentality to survive.

5. Black and Proud is not an aggressive chant. It is a positive statement.

 - 22nd October 2022

Chapter 21:
Let's Really Talk –
Gender Violence

SAFETY FIRST

I was meant to write about my visit 'home' to Nigeria, but hopefully I'll do that next week. Urgent matters have come up. I read again another report of a woman killed in her home by a partner. There has been so many of them this year.

In the UK, 1 in 4 women are affected by domestic violence. It can be physical, emotional, financial, sexual and coercive. It has led to the death of many women in our communities. The impact of domestic violence on children is even more damaging and shows up many years later in depression, anxiety, and substance misuse.

Research shows that violence in the home increases substantially during holidays and festive seasons. As we prepare for the Christmas holidays, let's reflect on what this could mean for some women. There is a lot of pressure on households and relationships. Add to that the pressures of the economic challenges on every household as a result of the 'cost of living' crisis, we know we are heading towards a 'perfect storm'. I pray it passes by without the predicted impact.

The on-going FIFA World Cup is bound to create more tensions in the home for most women. Research shows that the combination of football and alcohol is a trigger for violence towards those who should be cherished and loved most.

25 November was The United Nations' (UN) International Day for the Elimination of Violence against Women. It is an occasion for governments, international organizations and non-governmental organizations to raise public awareness of violence against women. It has been observed on November 25 each year since 2000.

The global theme for this year's 16 Days of Activism against Gender-Based Violence, which will run from 25 November to 10 December 2022, is "UNITE! Activism to end violence against women and girls". Please find out what is happening in your local area and support activities with donations or volunteering. For more info please go to;

https://16dayscampaign.org or
https://www.unwomen.org

For balance, I do acknowledge that men are also victims of domestic violence and it is not always about strength. But let's focus on the data and research. Women are more affected and are mostly the victims of intimate partner violence.

IF YOU HAVE EXPERIENCED DV, PLEASE REMEMBER;

- Your safety and that of your children should be your number one priority
- leave if you have to – don't go back without counselling and mediation
- Seek help. Please.

FOR CONFIDENTIAL ADVICE PLEASE CONTACT

In the UK:

Women's Aid at http://www.womensaid.org.uk

or Refuge at http://www.refuge.org.uk

In Nigeria:

For general safety advice and information;

Lagos State Domestic and Sexual Violence Agency at http://www.lagosdsva.org

or Project Alert at http://www.projectalertnig.org

Don't be a victim. Don't be a perpetrator.

My post was ready but has come late as I have been 'home' since the weekend. Long story to explain my late post, but hopefully back on track this weekend.

- 30th November 2022

Chapter 22:

My First Fog

My first writer's fog. I don't know what triggered it but then I realised yesterday, 15 October, was a possible trigger. We all have personal milestone dates that mean things to us, both good and bad. The bad may be linked to an emotional trauma, like mine. It could also have been work and study stress. I really can't be sure. But I'm not allowing such emotions clip my wings. We keep flying.

It took me a good two days to come out of the mind fog and emotional low - longer than usual. Thanks to my repertoire of tools - mindfulness, breathing exercise, mood scents, lights therapy, positive exposures and faith affirmations, among others, I came out of it in the end and that's why you're reading this blog; albeit a day later than my usual weekly Saturday morning postings. It's also coincidental that it happened in the week of World Mental Health Day, which I highlighted last week. By the way, October 13 was also International Skeptics Day. Who makes up these 'Days'! While they are at it, can we have 'I'm Losing The Will To Live Day? I digress.

I haven't done talking therapy sessions this year because, I felt I'd done so much in the last two years and that I was just being put through my therapist's own set of transformational methods, robotically. With my last therapist (I've used three, but I have my reasons), I didn't think it was empowering anymore. I felt I wasn't getting new energy after our sessions. Maybe, I felt she wasn't 'getting' me anymore. Maybe I knew myself better and was so much more aware of my anxiety and mental health issues. Maybe I didn't need a personal therapist anymore and was ready for another type of support. I don't know. There's also the cost. Seeing a therapist can be quite expensive, if you're funding it yourself, rather than through the NHS or your insurance. Anyway, I've stopped for now, and I think my own self-awareness coupled with informed response approach works for me.

While I've shared some of my battles with anxiety (just being able to do that is a biggie for me), my blog is not to focus purely on those battles. I'm not sure I can even be that fully open yet (some people might feel shocked to read the reality and impact of their actions), neither do I want to make my blog a 'one trick pony'. Besides, I'm still fearful and anxious of the negative aspects of social media - the trolling, dislikes, unkind comments, etc. I'm still on a path to knowing exactly what I want to project on this blog. Who do I want to be? Which part of me do I want to present? Do I reveal more of the personal, emotional, social, professional or academic side of me?

I certainly hope to use all these aspects to reflect on various issues of life and society; to empower, educate and care. I definitely won't keep mute about my anxieties and life experiences because, it is me. Not all anxieties are bad - some can be because we care too much about others. We love deeply. I'm still on the journey of life and, of course, I like to write and share. But hopefully, it will not be all doom and gloom. After all, this blog is about having an Audacious Life - vibrant, empowering, sassy, fun and bold.

If you are feeling emotionally low or anxious about life or a particular issue; please seek help or talk to someone you are comfortable with. You don't have to live it alone. There are also lots of resources available online.

Trust me, there's no embarrassment in seeking help. I did. Princes Harry and William did. Like many others, we're better for it today. We know, our 'why' and 'what'. We've been empowered and supported to live a more Audacious Life. So can you.

- 16th October 2022

Chapter 23:

Christmas v Festivity

It's almost here. What we've all been counting down for. One more sleep to Christmas.

I still find it fulfilling waking up Christmas morning. There's still that child-like excitement that I get. That soon evaporates when I think of all the cooking that needs to be done. I love Christmas. What irks me is what happens before and in the process of doing Christmas.

Let me pitch my guiding faith here but I won't be too heavy. Jesus is the reason for Christmas (clue is in the word). Why have we turned it into a frenzy of shopping excess and overspending?

I respect other faiths and gladly celebrate with friends when special dates come up. It's not a cliché for me that some of my closest friends are Muslims. My birth son's father for instance. However, I don't see the over commercialisation of these faith based events or dates – for instance Eid, Diwali or Hanukkah.

Christmas trees, Easter eggs, these are signs of Christmas or Easter celebrations but they have no connection with the actual Christian event. Muslims kill rams at Eid but that's because it IS part of what happened. The Holy Prophet sacrificed a ram in place of his son. Generations of the faithful have continued to do that in remembrance.

Despite my rant, I'm not going to be Scrooge today. Across the world, Christmas–like New Year–is a joyful time for most people, irrespective of creed or colour. It is a time we can pause before the year comes to an end. It prepares our mind for the New Year.

FIVE THINGS TO REMEMBER AT CHRISTMAS.

1. We may not all be able to splash out on Christmas like previous years, but give thanks for what you have and are blessed with. No matter how small or how it may compare with others, it's your way. Enjoy.

2. Christmas time is for family. We come together and put our family squabbles aside for one day. I know it's easier said than done, but we have to try. Those who have lost loved ones or spending the first Christmas without them, I wish you peace and comfort at this time.

3. Remember the less privileged and increase your giving to the poor. Christmas is a time of giving to the needy. We can all do it. Your time spent on helping others is also a way of 'giving'. Even an hour of your time has value. Many volunteers are needed at this time to support charities working with the homeless and rough sleepers. You can also volunteer with local charities to deliver food to the elderly and vulnerable in your areas.

4. Think of those in your community that don't have family, friends or food. If you can, invite them into your home, or share what you have.

5. Enjoy the day in the way that suits you best. My family setup is complicated, so for the last few Christmases I've tended to have a quiet 'me time' with good food, screen chats/video calls with friends/family, and watching my backlog of Netflix films. Same again tomorrow; I prefer it, for now. So, you can eat and chill with others or do it your way. If you can't be perfect, Be Kind.

Wishing you all a wonderful and happy Christmas.

- 24th December 2022

Chapter 24:
End Of Year: Rule 101

Wow, last day of 2022. What a year. A year of twos. Shall we call it a year of double trouble or double blessings.

For me, it was a year that I finally did many things I've been putting off for years. Yes, started my blog and have maintained it consistently. Also wrote my first book – watch out for it soon. Went back to Uni. Experienced new peace and energy to do more. I can only be grateful that this year made up for the last few years of turmoil and anxiety.

As a nation, we lost a Queen and gained a King. We just lost Pele and England didn't win the World Cup – hey, 2026 will give us another chance. We had the unusual situation of three Prime Ministers in one year. We had the 'freakiest' weather (hot and cold) on record. I can only imagine what temperatures we will get in 2023.

For some countries it has been an 'annus horribilis', – a year of disaster or misfortunes; a phrase famously used by our late Queen to describe her year in 1992, after the fire at Windsor Castle. This has indeed been an 'annus horribilis' for the people of Ukraine. I'm still stunned by what is going on there. I can't understand why the other super powers can't just STOP it. It shows that there are superpowers and then Superpowers.

I came across a really positive quote via one of my favourite YouTubers, Tayo Aina. He used a very relatable quote from a Portuguese poet, Fernando Pessoa about living in the present. It goes, 'I always live in the present.

The future I can't know. The past I no longer have'. Surely this is the wisdom of age for today, as we prepare to enter a new year.

Through my blog, I've tried to share some wisdom gained from my own personal experiences and lessons learnt from others. The number 101 can represent a time of new beginnings and growth. It is also a slang term for the most basic knowledge in some subject, as in "boiling eggs is cooking 101. To end the year, I'm sharing my personal best lessons from 2022 for an Audacious Life.

RULE 101 FOR END OF YEAR AND BEYOND.

1. Just show up – don't avoid. Show up at that party, gym, church, or friend's home. Accept those social invites to meet up and do things with others. Don't isolate. You can do it. You'll be amazed at how much fun it can be. All those initial fears will just be forgotten.

2. Don't avoid issues/problems or taking steps because of fear, but do it because you believe in it. Let that be your push for success and meeting your goals for 2023 and beyond.

3. You CAN start again, if you surround yourself with the right people or influences. The key is to reflect, review and refresh your plans. Learn from the last try or actions and avoid any stumbling blocks or

people. Be honest what or who those are – yourself included. This will move you closer to your goals and outcomes. We sometimes hinder our own plans without knowing. For example, you want to get a job in a particular sector or plan a career change. Have you checked your skills set against what is needed? Do you have to re-train? Is it an achievable goal for this phase of your life or age?

4. You can't avoid procedural processes or functional system order. Follow due process and order as it's a crucial step; then back it with prayer for speed, grace and favour. For example, you can't travel without a passport – no matter how much you try; ask many disappointed travellers. You need a passport, but prayers and favour/luck can make your journey much more pleasant and even better than planned; ask those who got a free flight upgrade without asking.

5. The mind is the greatest prison, if we don't open it to what is the truth. Have your own views about who you are as a person. You can be different. We don't need herd mentality to survive.

6. As a person of colour, don't just be taught your history but seek it yourself. Put a visit to Africa

or your country of heritage, in your bucket list. Experiencing or seeing it is better than reading, hearing about it or watching it on a screen.

7. It's Ok not to be OKAY. But take steps or seek help to deal with what's not making you OKAY. Ok.

8. Self-awareness and self-care is essential to live the life YOU love.

9. Be genuinely KIND to others – it is the only act that there is no justified law against… think about it!

10. What's your Rule 101 for 2023. Please add.

Life is what you make it. Go for it. I wish you all an 'annus mirabilis', – a wonderful year ahead.

- 31st December 2022

Chapter 25:

Tribute – Elizabeth II: Faith. Family. Friend

I read it somewhere that a life that has not been tested – whether that be through grief, disappointment, rejection, abuse or any other type of pain/trauma – such life cannot be fully known or determined. You don't know how a person will act towards these facets of life, until it happens to them. But what gets you through life is what I call the 'F' Factors – Faith, Family or Friends. Ideally all three.

As we her loyal subjects, along with other nations, mourn the immense loss of our beloved queen, Her Royal Majesty Queen Elizabeth II, let us look to these essential factors of life to see us through this period of grief and sadness.

Life tests can come in many ways. We can't avoid it, and if we live a life without it, we can't grow. Whether the test is from relationships, financial limits, challenging health or just a hard life. What you believe or hold on to, is what will see you through.

A royal life or one born into great wealth doesn't protect you from being tested. Her Majesty the Queen had her fair share of tests. From losing her father and becoming Queen at a young age, to having to be a support for her subjects in times of national tragedies and world events. Her own personal life and family came not without its own tests. The loss of her rock and husband, Prince Phillip. The loss of her younger sister, Margaret. The marriages of her children. The bad choices made by those she loved or trusted. I could go on. One thing I discovered over the years, is her inherent dependence on the 'F' Factors of Faith, Family and Friendships.

Faith can be a mystery. It is different for many religions, cultures and societies. But faith is faith, no matter the colour or creed. Faith is the assurance of receiving what we hope for but have not yet seen. It can be the difference between expecting and giving up. It can be reassuring as well as excruciating while we wait for our desired change. It can be weak or strong. It may not exist for some. Faith is like a fragrance. We can sense it but not always touch. But when it is strong, everyone can notice it on you, like a strong perfume. Faith can wipe away tears, heal, bless and restore peace. It renews strength for another day. It's an essential ingredient for a good and Audacious Life. Without a doubt, Queen Elizabeth II was a woman of great faith and it showed.

Family. It's also said that we can't choose our family. Some may wish they could. Whatever the view. Family is a fact of who we are. It gives us our identity at birth, develops our character along the way, and can give us a soft life or bumpy ride. Family meant everything to Her Majesty. She also had many tests with her immediate family members - some we knew. Many we may never have heard or read about. She also clearly had many joyful family moments and occasions. One vivid memory I have is during Prince Edward's wedding. The

Queen momentarily ignored queenship and quickly trotted after Edward and Sophie as they rode away from the church in their carriage. She was waving and beaming like any other mother who was seeing her last child get married. That said it all.

Friends we can choose. The right friendships can make all the difference in life. The Queen is known to have sustained many of her childhood friends to the very end. She chose well, and it showed in her life. No negative stories about her personal life hit our media. Her friends protected her like a shield and made life 'normal'. I'm sure there must have been many 'girls' night outs'. I hope so.

The 'F' Factor that nobody should live life with is Fear. However, one that we all need to frequently apply to life is Forgiveness. Indeed, these are often the two most difficult factors in life. Her Majesty the Queen, represented all three 'desirable 'F' Factors. She was also Fearless in her actions and dedication to duty. She was forgiving to those we may have considered not worthy of such acts.

As for Faith, she was Defender and Head of the Church of England. As Family, she was not just a mother to her children but also numerous subjects and many nations. As Friend, she welcomed everyone with a friendly smile and made the most nervous feel at ease. I'm privileged to have met her, albeit from a distance at one of her summer garden parties at Buckingham Palace. Her Majesty was a rare being that the United Kingdom may not see again. Her selfless dedication to duty will never be forgotten. We thank you Your Majesty for your life-long service and dignity in dealing with every situation and test that life brought you. You truly lived a good and Audacious Life.

Your Royal Majesty Queen Elizabeth II, by the Grace of God, of the United Kingdom of Great Britain and Northern Ireland and of other Realms and Territories Queen, Head of the Commonwealth, Defender of the Faith. Rest in perfect peace and rise in even greater majestic glory.

Kabiyesi, Iya wa, Mama Charles e sun re. Odun a ji na sira oooo! (Our Queen, our mother, mother of Charles, rest in perfect peace).

- 10th September 2022

Chapter 26:
Kings And Queens

CORONATION

It is said, heavy is the head that wears the crown. Indeed. Today saw the coronation of our new King of the United Kingdom – England, Wales, Scotland and parts of Ireland. It's been a long journey for this particular king. Charles III, as he will be officially known. His mother reigned for seventy years before her death. That's not a feat our new King is likely to achieve.

Not all of us can inherit a kingdom but sure as day, we all have a life purpose. We all become kings and queens when we fulfil our life purpose. It's said that life is give and take. It isn't always simultaneous. Life can take away your joy, but it can also give you plenty to celebrate – marriage, children, and good health. Some we take for granted.

We can allow what life takes from us to forget our purpose, or we can rise above it. Charles III waited seventy years to be crowned king. He knew it was coming from the time he became heir to the throne at four years old. He could have become resentful for the long wait. He could have given up for an easier life, but he knew his purpose had to be fulfilled. It didn't come without challenges. There is Diana. The delicate matter of adultery (on both sides). Then a child that breaks your heart despite all you've done for him.

Many of us have to wait for something that has been promised us or that we believe we are entitled to. Let us have the patience and dedication of Charles to wait.

For Charles III, it's not yet over, neither will his reign be like his mother's – our much-missed Queen Elizabeth II. He will be reigning over a diverse and multicultural country. Two of his current First Ministers are from ethnic minorities. This is a different Britain to the one his mother successfully ruled over. Subjects are less tolerant and reverent to the throne. Whatever your leanings, Royalist or Republican, let us reflect and appreciate what I can only describe as an amazing Coronation. Will I see William crowned? Who knows. May the years be many before the next Coronation.

Charles, III we welcome your reign over us your subjects. As we say in my country of heritage, *'Ade a pe lori. Bata a pe lese'* May the Crown remain long on your head. May the royal slippers remain long on your feet. *'Kaaaaabiyesi oooo. Ashe'*. Long live the King. Amen.

- 6th May 2023

Chapter 27:
Coronation Reflections

A LIFE OF SERVICE

Recently, a weekend without a bank holiday feels strange. Some might still be recovering from the last one. Most probably our newly crowned King is too!

Wasn't the coronation something. Where did you watch it? Please share. It's one of those occasions that in twenty years' time, you can usually remember where you were on the day. I chose to spend the Coronation weekend in Canterbury. I was able to watch the Coronation live streamed inside the famous Cathedral. It really made it extra special. At the start, I really didn't know what to expect. Never witnessed a monarch being crowned before. What stood out for me was how the anointing was kept sacred and the King shielded from view for it. In this day of live streaming and reporting, it was good to see something kept away from the cameras.

This was an event steeped in tradition but uniquely updated to reflect the Britain of today. From the bearers of the King's regalia of office - gloves, rings, etc, who were chosen to represent and recognise the diverse ethnic citizens and different faiths that successfully co-exist in Britain today. While it remains a predominately Christian nation - reflected in the beautiful Coronation of King Charles III, this particular change to the ceremony was a unique way of incorporating other faiths by The Defender of The Faith. That's a separate history lesson folks! I absolutely loved seeing a woman carry the King's sword, and so fiercely too. Superwoman came second to Penny M, that day.

The key message about all this was poignantly made at the start of the ceremony when a little boy welcomed the King and he responded 'I come not to be served but to serve'. In an age where it's about individual relevance, likes or influences, this was a great reminder that we are all called first to serve and every other thing we desire will be added to us. At the late Queen's funeral all the regalia and treasures of her status were removed from her coffin, one by one. The Crown, the Sceptre, the Orb, and she was buried without them. They reappeared for the crowning of the new King and were added to him after his declaration to serve and his anointing. That is a deep reflection of life to think about.

When you serve and give to others - whether that's money or your time; there is a marked change to you. This has been proved medically and theologically. Our new King has given us all a challenge to serve - in small and big ways. You can start with kindness. You choose, but please choose and just do it. A life of service leads to an Audacious Life. Think about it.

LAST WORD

If we can honour a man like this, Lord how must we honour you… with body and with mind. Amen.

- 14th May 2023

Part Two:
NIGERIAN LIFE

Chapter 28:
It's Complicated
— Naijabrit

Life can be complicated, even more so as a Nigerian-British. What do I mean. Basically, you live in the UK but you regularly have to balance your British life with the influences and norms of your birth country or parental heritage, culture and society. Mine is balancing my British life with my Nigerian heritage – hence my coined NaijaBrit identity and realisation. I'm laying it out here so you will understand the blend in my writings, words and life reflections.

Being a NaijaBrit is unique. It doesn't necessarily mean you were born in the UK. You could have been born in Nigeria. You can hold citizenship of either country, or even both. What makes you a NaijaBrit is being comfortable in both societies, cultures and norms. You easily say 'bawoni, 'kedu' or 'Asalam' when you meet Naija friends. But you just as easily say 'innit' when you need your Brit friends to agree with you on something.

I'm proudly NaijaBrit. I was born in Nigeria. Spent first five years of life there. Arrived in England and spent ten. Moved back to Nigeria for another five years. Came back to England and have lived here ever since. I've lived in the UK more years than I lived in Nigeria, but I visit Nigeria a lot and love both societies. But it's complicated and sometimes feels like having a split personality. It makes you respectful but also assertive at the same time – especially when you get frequent requests for money. I sometimes think in my native language, then struggle to explain it in English because I can't find the right or proper translation – or vice versa. I have to explain to my Brit friends when I say, I'm going 'home for Christmas'. You get it.!

FIVE SIGNS YOU'RE A NAIJABRIT
(AUDACIOUS LIFE VERSION!)

1. You lived the majority of your life in the UK but spent at least five years of your education in Nigeria.

2. You know the difference between black pudding and Yorkshire pudding. The difference between Gala and sausage roll. The difference between *'owambe'* and a party.

3. Your accent and language regularly and easily 'switches' from Queens/Cockney/London, to urban Nigerian language/accent/slangs.

4. You're known/called mostly by your Nigerian name by family/friends but known only by your English or adapted Nigerian name (Lara to Laura, Bamidele to Bami, etc), at work or by Brit friends. The two are often different personalities.

5. You like wearing designer 'labels' and listening to urban or soul music, but also love rocking local African fabric designs and dancing to Afrobeats or *'Wasiu'*.

If you failed to meet the mark, you're an Honorary NaijaBrit, if you tick any one of these identifiers;

- You've tried Nigerian *jollof*, *fufu* and *egusi*. Love it and eat it regularly – at home, in restaurants, or as takeouts.

- You understand your parents' native language or at least all the key words, sentences, phrases, and slangs. Even if you can't speak it fluently.

- You have attended more than five Nigerian weddings anywhere in the world.

- You can dance Afrobeat with swagger and sing the lyrics with abandon (your full chest..!)

What makes YOU a NaijaBrit? … please tell.

- 3rd September 2022

Chapter 29:
Blended Families – Blended Bliss

My father died in 2021. His life would need a book to tell. But one thing he created is a family with so many dimensions of half-siblings, step-mothers, step-brothers and sisters. It's a challenge maintaining family relationships, but I do my best.

They say we can't choose our family. I think that has changed. As a NaijaBrit, I grew up having to call anyone who was a friend of my parents as Aunty or Uncle. A knock on the head came swiftly if you tried to do otherwise and call them by name. My white 'Oyinbo' friends couldn't understand why I had so many aunties, uncles and cousins. Neither could I, initially. But I soon appreciated the wonderful friends and relationships it brought into my life and maintained till today.

Let me share a bit. I have ten half-siblings but I didn't grow up with most of them. It's only since my father died that we've been trying our best to build sibling relationships. But it hasn't been easy.

For many years, most people I have a very strong bond with and introduce as my 'sisters' (Aunty D, Funmi, Layo) are not. We share neither blood nor relatives – but you can't tell. We became family through integration and association. We grew up together, shared significant milestones, and gradually blended in and got accepted by parents and siblings as part of the family. When you can go to a Nigerian friend's home and enter the kitchen to dish your own food, then you've become family. Can we call this African adoption. I have.

Blended families are being created in every society. We can look to the Trump family being infused by the recent wedding of his daughter to a Naija-bred Lebanese young man. We can look even more closer to see the blended families in the Royal family. King Charles and Camilla. Princess Beatrice and her step-son. Royal Family trees will never be the same again.

On the flip side of blended families is blended wahala (stress/trouble). We only have to look to Harry and Megan's on-going Netflix series. Wow, a masterclass in how it can all go wrong. I won't say more than that. I want to remain optimistic that blended families enrich lives.

So here I am preparing to go to one of my 'sons' wedding introduction. This stage of the Nigerian wedding process is usually only for nuclear family but hey, I'm family – blood or no blood.

Kika, our new and beautiful Duchess, welcome to our family. We are blessed to have you.

- 10th December 2022

Chapter 30:

Be Prepared
– Going Home

I'm off to my much loved Nigeria (or Naija, as I prefer) this week, for the marriage introduction ceremony of one of my 'sons'. I always say if I know when you were born, changed your pampers more than a few times, know most of the schools you attended, present at most of your milestone events and still have that bond of friendship with your parents; then you're my child. I have many 'children' and quite a few just happen to be sending me notice of their weddings. 2023 is gonna be expensive for me. But we are prepared. No shaking.

Be prepared is the famous Scout Motto, which means you are always in a state of readiness in mind and body to do your duty. Allow me to paraphrase that to 'readiness in mind and body to travel to Nigeria', if you live in the diaspora, like me.

Travelling to Nigeria at any time requires serious planning, and some even say courage. From what to pack, to who will pick you at the airport, and to how you will stay safe. Anxiety over all the 'bad' news and scary stuff. I know it's a challenging time but which country doesn't have its problems right now. I aim to always remain positive. I won't keep away.

I've used the Scouts motto to literally reduce anxiety about going home at this time. However, it can be applied to all aspects of life; especially at this time of recession and worries for the future. *Koni baje*. We keep moving. Higher, higher. Buga oooo!

FIVE TIPS FOR TRAVELLING TO NIGERIA/NAIJA

1. Packing is a process that starts weeks before travel. You can't pack in one day. As a seasoned traveller, trust me. I usually bring my suitcases out at least three weeks before and just throw things in as I remember. I then arrange and re-arrange in the week of travel. You need time to gather all the things required for specific visits. Are you going for relaxation, to visit family, for an occasion – birthday, wedding, funeral etc. Each requires different items to pack. That's also separate to all the 'basics' you need to carry oooo! I know it's easier now with Shoprite and other well-stocked supermarkets, but if you don't want to be hunting round for your preferred toothpaste, coffee or gadget accessories, please buy and pack. You know just what you absolutely must have to make your visit less stressful.

2. Have a first day pack for when you arrive. It will save you scattering suitcases to find items you need on arrival. It will be different for everyone, but it also depends on if you're staying in your own home, with family or in a hotel. Mine usually contains medicine, coffee/tea sachets, house keys, mobile

internet device, personal door alarm and possibly some breakfast items like oats and jam. It's easier to get main meals as takeaways, until you settle and can do your own cooking.

3. Please check and follow any requirement or travel protocol imposed by the government of the country you are going, especially if it's to Nigeria. It will save you a lot of begging or shouting at your departure and arrival airport. Trust me. Please check official websites, but also lots of helpful YouTube travel videos on latest issues to guide you.

4. Not everyone needs to know. I say this not because of 'village people' mentality, or people who will plan to harm you or disrupt your plans. No. It's because it will reduce the number of requests to 'bring this, bring that'. It will help with your packing and hopefully ensure that you don't have unnecessary or excessive luggage. Airlines are not smiling since the losses of the pandemic. You can beg all you like but you will be asked to pay or take stuff out, if you go over the limit, even by one Kg. It's okay paying for excess luggage if you've planned for it, but to have excess luggage because of biscuits and tea from UK, requested by 'Aunty', is a no, no. Some friends and family even ask for basic things like deodorant and apples or things easily bought in good supermarkets in

Nigeria. So annoying. Easier to show love in other ways and with cash.

5. You can't please everyone. Yes that's right and don't try to - you'll just be stressed out, even before you get on that plane. Be intentional and focus on the purpose of your visit. Who do you need to, or MUST see. Some people you've not told of your visit may hear from others and be annoyed. A call can replace an actual visit to extended family or friends. Manage expectations/situations with care and respect at all times. Living abroad doesn't push you to the top of your family tree. You will always have elders and other people to honour. You can't please everyone, but you need to know who to prioritise and keep on your side. You might have more cash than some (depends on your background and family situation) but avoid creating unnecessary tensions for yourself.

If you are planning to 'travel home' for Christmas, please plan and be careful or in Naija urban parlance, 'be sharp', and 'open ya eyes well, well'.

Most especially have fun, enjoy the awesome cuisines and try not to 'shayo' or get drunk - Nigerian alcohol is super strong! There's no place like 'home' for Christmas, or at any time, actually.

- 19th November 2022

Chapter 31:
Nigerian Weddings

BE PREPARED

I've been in Nigeria for just over a week now. For Easter and The Wedding. I said before that attending a Nigerian wedding needs to be on everyone's bucket list. I've been to many, but none made me as emotional as this one. It was one of my Bond Friend's son getting married. He's just like my son too. The joy of seeing a young person who you helped nurture from birth, surely comes on a level only after the parents. This particular wedding was a slightly new cultural experience as the bride is from another tribe in Nigeria – making the occasion even more vibrant. It was also nice to see some friends that I hadn't seen for a while, and we sure had a swell time. Still recovering from it all – hence another late blog. It's allowed.

You know me, I always like to have something to take away from any life experience. That's why we have an Audacious Life. From this particular wedding it wasn't just the amazing goody bags that I took. Here's my take.

FIVE THINGS TO KNOW ABOUT NIGERIAN WEDDINGS

1. **Be prepared.** Yes oooo. From getting group fabric (*aso ebi*) designed to the highest possible standards. It's easier said than done. Trust me. Some Nigerian tailors are on par with Nigerian politicians and UK Estate Agents – they can mess you up. An outfit that is supposed to be ready

at least a day to the wedding party may not be ready until after nuptials have been concluded, if at all. There are a thousand stories that can be told. Thankfully my tailor didn't disappoint. I know many who did. Then after all that palava over your outfit, there's the shoes, bag, nails, makeup, and *gele*/headtie to be sorted. Everyone wants to be the belle of the party.

2. **There will be other outfits that stand out more than yours.** After all your efforts, you may not even make it to the top ten best dressed. Trust me. What looks, sassy, freaky or couture in your mirror or at your designer's fitting room; will have stiff competition on the day. But hey, that shouldn't be an issue for anyone who has an Audacious Life attitude. After all, we know who we are and confident in our own skin – not what we wear. Yeah. Good; let's keep moving.

3. **Don't get easily offended.** Very important. Naija weddings are stressful – make that ALL weddings. Everyone is on high tension or worried about plans going wrong. From the parents of the couple to the caterers of the day. So don't like a friend did at another wedding, walk out of the venue because the bride's mother didn't greet you well. Sometimes a celebrant can be overwhelmed on the day with playing a major role in the ceremony

to also having to keep an eye on the things going on around them. So if they don't smile or hug you as you walk in; they may just be overwhelmed at that particular moment. Give them time. They will be more relaxed as the ceremony progresses. If you didn't get the right meal or your table didn't get served choice wines or 'small chops', don't get angry. It may likely be a mistake and not that others are being treated better or as VIPs. If food has finished early or it wasn't enough, don't get upset. You're there to celebrate. Pick up some takeaway food on your way home. I always make sure I eat something before going to an event – just in case. If you didn't get wedding souvenirs or goody bags, you can let who invited you know and I'm sure they will get one for you. If not, it's not the end of the world. I can bet you already have the same items at home already. If not, come to my house to collect. Lol.

4. **It's not about you.** Yes. If you're a wedding guest, it's not. It's the bride, groom and their parents' day. You're there to support and rejoice with them. So when they ask you to stand to pray, you do. It's not a time to be talking. When you're asked not to crowd the couple as they are dancing, you don't. When you're asked to wait for tables to be called before going for food. You wait. If the MC or live musician/

singer didn't acknowledge your presence at the event, remember it's not about you.

5. **Be kind and thoughtful.** Very important and an essential aspect of having an Audacious Life. Kindness and thoughtfulness to others. From the celebrants to those that are serving. Everyone has their role and are trying to do it well. Appreciate it in every way. Show kindness to those that serve your table and bring your food or drinks. Without them, the wedding may be more stressful for you as a guest. Be courteous and thoughtful to security – they are only doing their jobs. So be Kind.

Seun and Kika, wishing you both a blessed and joyful marriage.

- 16th April 2023

Chapter 32:

*Airegin
– Hard Life 2*

What is 'Airegin'. Keep reading, you'll soon find out. I've been referring to my visit to Nigeria in past posts. I've been here a week now. Do I feel it! When I wrote a few weeks ago lamenting about how life has become so hard in UK, I didn't know that was 'small matter' compared to the issues I met in Nigeria. This is the hardest life. I say this not to joke but to describe what people are going through right now.

The first shock that I met was the crippling petrol shortage. This was on a scale worse than I've known before because of the price increases making it unaffordable for most. So in areas where petrol is being sold at the 'official rate' (God bless those businesses), the crowds there were stadium numbers. Roads near such petrol stations became a nightmare to pass through, leading to traffic in my beloved city of Abeokuta – a rare thing. It is not Lagos. We came to Abeokuta to avoid traffic oooo.

In Nigeria, fuel is what drives the economy. So when there is petrol shortage, everything goes up. Food, transport and having electricity in your home to keep cool (70 percent of the time we have to buy fuel and use our own generators). What was so heartbreaking was seeing the large numbers of school kids and workers having to trek long distances in the searing heat to get to their destinations, as there were hardly any taxis or motorbikes to transport them.

The impact on businesses is unimaginable. Even some fast-food outlets that normally have chilled air conditioning inside their premises, have turned these off and now open doors and windows – I kid you not. Taxis (if you can get one), now give two costs for their services. With air conditioning, you pay more. Less without. So, it was open windows for me oooo!

The government of Nigeria recently revealed that about 63 percent of people living in Nigeria (133 million) are living in poverty.

This came from research carried out by internal and external agencies including UNICEF and the Oxford Poverty and Human Development Initiative (OPHI). We should all take this research seriously and reflect on how our leaders have failed us.

56,000 households across the 36 states of Nigeria were sampled in the research which was conducted between November 2021 and February 2022.

The report states that over half of the population of Nigeria are multidimensionally poor and cook with dung, wood or charcoal, rather than cleaner energy. High deprivations are also apparent nationally in sanitation, healthcare, access to food, and housing. This is extremely sad data.

There was a country called Nigeria but what we have now is 'Airegin' – Nigeria going backwards.

Today, I really don't have points or advice to give. I'm stunned and dumbfounded. God help my much loved Nigeria. I know transformational change is coming, good or bad. I pray for a good and peaceful change. We need it.

- 3rd December 2022

Chapter 33:

What Next
– What's The Legacy?

Who do you look up to? What's your motivation? How do you recognise success? Is it who the world tells you? Think again, because isn't it canny how some Forbes Listed or cover people are being revealed as fraudsters and scammers. The latest is Theranos founder, Elizabeth Holmes, who just got an eleven-year jail sentence for fraud. We had our own Nigerian example, Obi Okeke, known as Invictus Obi, who was on the same Forbes cover at one time as Forbes under 30. He got ten years for fraud last year. Supposed Crypto king, Sam Bankman-Fried is also waiting to be served his own desserts. Who's clapping now.

I've just come back from Nigeria and I'm greatly motivated to do even more for others in need. The poverty level is unprecedented for this nation that I know so well. Yes, we have people who are extremely rich and can hire Onassis's yacht to celebrate a birthday (not knocking FO, he's a giver too) but they are in the minority. Social media can gloss over people's reality. Besides, Nigerians are known to be happy people. We don't let problems stop the fun or parties. Everyone has their levels.

But this trip was different. The need was more visible. People I know to be comfortable, were even complaining about the impact of the economy on their business and ability to do normal stuff - pay school fees, fuel cars and generators, etc. If they feel it, how much more low-income earners, small traders or manual labourers. No wonder the rate of *'japa'* by the middle class and skilled professionals, is now noticeably high.

A lot is going on across the world right now – not just the extreme weather in both hot and cold countries. As we prepare for Christmas, the demand on families is huge. We that are able to give – either to people back 'home' or here in the UK, need to start thinking about giving back and to also consider our own legacy. It's time.

I founded a charity in Nigeria about five years ago, to channel my giving back and also encourage others to do same. I was motivated to establish the NGO after accompanying a church pastor on welfare visits to homes of sick members from his congregation. It was disturbing to discover the impact of what being sick and having no sickness pay can do to a household's finances – even temporarily. There is no state welfare. This motivated me to initially set up a 'crisis fund' to help people in need. This later emerged to full registration and establishment of Phebe Benevolent Foundation. I'm extremely proud of the impact we've made and continue to make to support those in crisis need.

We all can't set up NGOs. Legacy is not always about structures, but can be built on kindness. We can support the charities that we know function well (there are a lot of suspicious ones oooo, so do your research and diligence).

FIVE WAYS YOU CAN HELP TO END OR REDUCE THE IMPACT OF POVERTY IN OUR COMMUNITIES.

1. Give to help empower communities around the world in order to create lasting change by donating to charities working with the poorest communities or groups.

2. Sponsor a child to help equip them with access to essentials such as clean water, healthcare, economic opportunity, and quality education. For less than $40 a month, you'll help that child and their community to stand tall, free from poverty.

3. For list of NGOs and community groups working in Nigeria, please visit http://www.nnngo.org to find a suitable NGO to support.

4. Please support food banks and homeless charities at this time. For list of charities in the UK, please check http://www.charitychoice.co.uk or Charity Commission's website

5. Learn more about actions to end extreme poverty. What are governments and world agencies doing. Check UNICEF and similar bodies.

- 17th December 2022

Chapter 34:
Home & Away

WHERE IS HOME?

I've been away. I'm back home now. Where is home. As a Naija-Brit who loves both Nigeria and England equally, I'm often asked by friends, 'which country do you prefer'. It's hard to choose because each country has its own relevance and ambience.

Clearly, England is my main country of residence for now, at this stage of life. It is where I work, raised my child, developed my career and professional relevance. It is where I have significant investments and personal footprints. It's where I've spent most of my life. It's my primary home.

Nigeria on the other hand has been a place to go for family occasions and have fun with long standing friends. It has always been a place to reconnect with being Black and relevant. A place to be physically seen as an equal to every other person. A place to escape from racism, discrimination and unconscious bias of living in Europe. A place to feel like a first-class citizen. It's not a perfect place – there's the high level of poverty in the society. The huge gap between rich and poor. The corruption and tribal disputes. Poor provision of electricity, water and infrastructure. The high crime rate and insecurity. Not an easy place to call 'home' but for me it is.

Sometimes it's like I have a double life. In England, I'm a 9-5 person and moulded into the typical routine of using public transport, suburban life and keeping to your social lane. Then there's the life in Nigeria where I have access to chauffeur driven cars, domestic staff and personal security. I can easily eat in the best restaurants and regularly attend social events where high-ranking government officials and high net worth individuals are in attendance. Some I know personally, or are relations. Such aspects of life can be difficult for a Black or minority ethnic person to experience in England, but thankfully times are changing and glass ceilings shattered on many levels – in government, in business and even titled aristocratic society. The labours of those before us have not been in vain.

More recently, as I'm nearing that stage of 'empty nest' and life becoming more slow paced; Nigeria draws me closer, as a place to renew life in older years. A place to escape the cold, isolation and loneliness that can overwhelm older people in England. Who doesn't want a life where it's sunny all year round and neighbours actually look out for you and are interested in your welfare. A place where there is always a family event or visits from friends. A place where older and elderly people are accorded respect because of their age. Most importantly, a place where your pension can get you more, than in England. I know even non-Africans seek to find a new 'home' for their twilight and retirement years. As we grow older, community begins to matter. We need to belong. We need a purpose. Where you find it is where you call 'home'.

LAST WORD:

Home is where the heart is. Audacious Life attitude means you are comfortable wherever you choose to be. We draw on knowing who we are from our lived experiences. We keep moving to fulfil our purpose, wherever we are.

- 23rd April 2023

Chapter 35:

Practice Makes Perfect

KEEP MOVING

A few weeks ago, I was lucky enough to be present during choir practice at a renowned cathedral outside London. I've never even witnessed my local church choir in practice. We just see perfection and orchestrated harmony of the singers and instrumentalists on Sundays. So, what a wonder to have an amazing behind the scenes experience. One thing that struck me was the number of times the choirmaster made singers and instrumentalists repeat and repeat parts of a song because he didn't think they were hitting the right notes. To me with an untrained ear, what was not good enough for the choirmaster, sounded just perfect. It made me think and connect with what is generally said about practice making perfect.

How does this relate to having an Audacious Life? It's about not giving up. It's about improving and developing. It's about not being put off by others who think you're okay where you are, have done enough, or ask what you are still looking for.

I was at an event yesterday, where we were celebrating African women who have made great strides in their career or amazing impact in their community and wider society. Every one of the awardees had made a mark and deserved their nominations. Let me say big shout to one of them. Lara Oyedele, is the first President of the Chartered Institute of Housing, from a BME background.

As a member of CIH (the professional body for UK Housing practitioners - so she is my President too), I know it's not a small achievement at all. Please check out her profile. I'm immensely proud. Thank you, Nigeria Magazine, for recognising her and all the other winners.

But the point I want to make about ALL the winners is that they were not candidates for such awards from day one of their working life. No. Along the way they must have had their own challenges - visible and not so obvious. We see the perfection of the practice and life lessons that they applied to get to what has made them stand out. It was so inspiring to listen to the bios and stories of the winners. It truly was a wonderful evening. One thing I always love about Naija blended events is the 'after party'. Yes oooo!, we can do the formal and professional stuff but once that part of an event is over, we move to the dance, dance, dance. Our professional and stoic ladies can dance. Even me 'shy mama', shook body. That's one thing I still need to perfect - my dancing!

We're all made perfect by our creator but after birth, life can become good, bad or complicated. We all pray for good. Our parents and elders pray, decree and declare a perfect life for us when we are born. However, life has its own plans; but practice makes perfect. Don't ever give up. Keep moving.

LAST NOTE

Clocks go forward tomorrow in the UK. Yaaaaay. Summer is almost here. Can't wait. Let me start bringing out my lovely African print dresses and enjoy the party season.

- 25th March 2023

Chapter 36:

Rainbow Life
v Mono Life

Rainbows mean many things to us. For some it is a sign of hope, promises and new beginnings. More recently, the rainbow colour has become the symbol of unity and equality.

A Rainbow Life is one that uses all that life has to offer and creates a life that impacts positively on all. While Mono Life is the opposite. It is a life ordinary. It focuses on me, myself and I. It acknowledges only those that we approve of, or are like us in nationality, heritage, class or ideology.

I've had been reflecting in the last few weeks about British life, as I often do. More so after the burial of our late Queen Elizabeth II. Wasn't it wonderful to see most countries of the world represented at her funeral. The sea of mourners from every ethnic group – white and black, lining up to see her lying in state, was an indication of her Rainbow life. Definitely a Rainbow funeral.

What makes Britain unique and different from other western countries is perhaps our diverse communities and willingness to integrate with people from other nations, cultures and religions. We have allowed people from far and near countries, to make the UK their home and for their future generations. I'm not saying it's been all smooth and we have totally integrated at all levels, but we have a right to aspire and we are seeing that emerging in all aspects of our society.

Having access to a rich and diverse commonwealth of nations, Britain has utilised such links effectively. How do we have such a rich Afro Caribbean community, if we didn't have Windrush? What about students who came from many developing nations to study in England and were able to stay and have their own families here? We now have third and fourth generation immigrant families. Their children are who we see in the public glare as politicians, civil servants, sports stars, actors, academics, and business entrepreneurs. We are present in all sectors and thankfully, now at the highest level of public life.

Just look at our government. Who didn't swell with pride to watch our new and first black Chancellor of the Exchequer, the Right Hon, Kwasi Kwarteng read out his first budget. I'll leave my comments on the outcome of that 'mad' budget for another day. But it doesn't take away his achievement of being 'The First'.

My other country, Nigeria is celebrating its Independence Day today, 1st October. It's been sixty two years since we gained independence from Britain. Have we become a nation of excellence? I leave you to evaluate that on other platforms or through political writers because you don't want to get me started. What I do know is that, Nigeria is a natural Rainbow Nation with rich diversity and cultures but sadly has been operating as a Mono Nation for many years. It's been a battle of one group or ethnic tribe wanting dominance and rights to leadership.

Next year we should be swearing in a new President, after elections which are due to start later this year. Some say we have a chance for the change that we need. I pray so.

FIVE PLEAS TO WHOEVER WILL BE LEADING NIGERIA FROM MAY 2023.

Dear Incoming Mr or Madam (why not!) President. Please, *'ejo'*, *'biko'*, try and ensure the following in your agenda and plans for my beloved Nigeria.

1. Protect the rights of every child to basic school education. This is a Human Right. It's clear enough.

2. Create a safe and enabling environment for young girls and women to live and flourish. Make more efforts to protect our young girls.

3. Pay a fair wage to all workers with a realistic minimum wage. There is too much hardship in the country, but it seems our politicians don't share the pain.

4. Use the best talents and skills to do the work of nation rebuilding. Nigeria has them in abundance. Ask Joe Biden, how he's using Nigerian talent and others to make America great again.

5. Lead by example. Be a servant friend. Nigeria cannot afford to keep getting it wrong with our

leaders. It's time to be humble and stop being monoethnic in the distribution of national wealth, privileges and positions.

Happy Independence Day. God bless Nigeria.

- 1st October 2022

Chapter 37:
It's Your Turn
— Eyin Lokan

CIVIC DUTY AND ELECTIONS

My country of heritage, Nigeria goes to the polls later this month, so this is going to be a long read..! We've had some crazy campaign slogans and speeches, but the one that raised the roof was *'E mi lokan'* – it's my turn. Most Nigerians know the genesis of this phrase, so I won't go into it, as I'm not here to promote any candidate. But let me use this loaded statement to paraphrase it to *'Eyin Lokan'* – it is YOUR turn.

The beauty of the Yoruba language is its versatility and how phrases written the same way, can be turned into a totally different meaning. *'E mi lokan'*, can also mean 'it concerns me'. Those who can write well in Yoruba will know (I can't). So as a passionate Nigerian, even though I'm not eligible to vote in the coming elections, the outcome of the 2023 elections, *e mi lokan* too. In fact, *'e mi lokan gan ni'* – it concerns me very much. We really must change election systems, to allow Diaspora votes just because of our sheer numbers.

We often say there's no place like home. This is absolutely true for Nigerians in Diaspora. As we grow older, we long for warmer climates and a place with strong community life and traditions that care for and respect the elderly. We need Nigeria to survive for us and future generations.

Currently, it's clear that Nigeria is in crises. No petrol. Limited access to cash due to the chaos caused by the redesign of Naira notes. No electricity, but that's nothing new to long-suffering citizens. We can't continue this way. The stories and urgent request for money from friends that don't usually ask, is alarming. It's getting harder to help, especially as we in the UK face our own economic challenges and cost of living crises.

Let's stop the rot that has created a country called **'Airegin' - Nigeria going backwards**. Let's get our country Nigeria back.

Nigeria is a nation still flowing with unlimited resources that can be used to make it one of the best countries in Africa. We were once on the right path but somehow lost our way. I'm grateful that I experienced the 'old' Nigeria, which was good, safe and fun. We had leaders who cared and had vision to make the country great for its citizens and provide leadership in the West African region. The records are there. When we moved back to Nigeria in 1980, the Naira value was at par with the Dollar. We may not get that back, but let's get back the basics for any country. Security, infrastructures, jobs and good governance.

If you've registered to vote, please go and get your PVC - voting card.

Whoever's turn it is to be our next President, please God, let that person be a 'game changer'. We need a multi-skilled leader who can motivate and hold those with assigned or elected responsibilities to account. We know it will take years to get Nigeria back on its feet. Let's not kid ourselves. It will require huge capital and possibly higher taxation. We all need to be prepared.

We can't all be leaders, but we have the unique opportunity to be a king maker.

Claim your Vote. Be the change maker. Vote wisely. *'Eyin Lokan'* – it's YOUR turn. *Awa Lokan'* – it's OUR turn.

- 4th February 2023

Chapter 38:
The D-Day

NIGERIAN ELECTIONS

I've never thought what D-Day actually meant, but I know it's generally associated with the Normandy landings that brought about the end of World War II. I checked to be sure and found that the D in D-Day also stands for Day. This coded designation was used for the day of any important invasion or military operations. I can relate to that. 25 February 2023 is our D-Day in Nigeria, my country of heritage. A nation much loved by me and many who live outside its shores but are connected to it in many ways. I don't usually discuss politics – it gives me a headache. But I have to talk about it today. Bear with me.

Nigeria's Presidential elections has taken place. I'm not sure who has decided – our votes or the violence, intimidation and outright electoral malpractices that has been reported or shared on various media platforms. Elections are generally held to give citizens a chance to choose a government for the people, by the people – the fundamentals of a democratic nation. What we've had in Nigeria in recent years is far from that. We have had successive governments that care less if citizens are unable to have basic human rights – those that make life worth living, such as the rights to food, education, work, health, and liberty. And it's been worse in the last decade. That's the soul wrenching truth and I can defend this assertion on any forum. Since the beginning of the year, most Nigerians have been unable to access money from banks. Unable to feed. Unable to educate their children. Unable to live a normal daily life. Yes, that bad.

Our hope has been focused on the 'coming elections', as an opportunity for citizens to use their votes wisely. I hope that is what has happened. While nobody has prayed for a military invasion of any kind, yesterday was surely Nigeria's D Day. A day for its citizens to root out corruption, malaise, nepotism and all expired politicians (those who were voted in based on their positive manifestos but failed to deliver). We still have other elections coming up in the next few weeks to elect Governors, etc. I pray we the people, will have the victory on our D Day. God bless Nigeria.

- 26th February 2023

Chapter 39:
The First Hurdle

AFTERMATH OF ELECTIONS – CALM DOWN!

The Nigerian Presidential elections are over. It didn't really feature in UK news bulletins but why would it; is Nigeria still the Giant of Africa? I'm keeping it going for another week. Be patient. I'm not getting political on you. We'll be back to lighter stuff soon. Promise.

We've crossed the first hurdle and elected the next President of Nigeria – we hope. Nothing is ever certain in politics. May handover date is still a few months away and legal challenges have already been filed in court. We even still have the Governorship elections to come next week. We watch and pray for the elections to be settled and for everyone to unite and rebuild Nigeria.

Whether you are a BATman, OBIdient or ATIKUlated, we have to move on. Some need to rebuild relationships with friends, family, neighbours and other tribes. Some people need to apologise for whipping up tribal sentiments and damaging reputations for selfish ambitions.

Some voters have mixed emotions. Some feel denied of their votes and outraged with the outcome. As one who wasn't eligible to vote in the Nigerian elections (hope I will for the next one – that's a goal), I can't say I know how some people feel. But I can relate to disappointment and unmet expectations. I know how this can limit thoughts and impact the drive for having an Audacious life. One of my friends is so upset that I'm having to tell her 'calm down'. I won't even mention election battles on WhatsApp group platforms that I'm on – thank goodness for mute and archive functions. I've dropped my mic on elections comments, and boohoos for now. Let others continue. I'm done.

You know that I'm a passionate advocate for well-being and mental wellness. It's my Rule 101 for an Audacious Life. So, I thrive on good vibes and focus on positive experiences. I was thinking of what lessons to share in relation to this and the impact of the elections but found someone who has already done that brilliantly. Why stress; no shame in borrowing wisdom and sense with acknowledged credits.

FIVE WAYS TO COPE IF YOUR CANDIDATE DIDN'T WIN THE ELECTION. (SOURCE: @DRGBONJUBOLAABIRI)

1. It's okay to be disappointed, frustrated, or sad if your candidate is not elected; acknowledge your feelings but don't let them overwhelm you.

2. Encourage yourself and others that you have done your part by casting your votes and focus on what you can control. Celebrate the power of democracy and the impact of your vote.

3. Even though your candidate didn't win, they may still be involved in the political process. Keep up with their work and stay engaged in the cause you both care about.

4. Mend the broken bridges or fences caused by the heated debates of the election campaign season. Reconcile differences and work together to build understanding and common ground.

5. Make sure to take time to rest, relax and practice self-care. Do activities you enjoy, and take breaks from news and election results.

- 4th March 2023

Chapter 40:

A New Dawn

INAUGURATION OF HOPE

If you're a blended NaijaBrit like me, you'll be excited about the week ahead. Not just because we have another bank holiday in England, but because Monday is also the inauguration of the new President of the Federal Republic of Nigeria, Bola Ahmed Tinubu.

I'll leave it to those who are more qualified than me to assess the success of the outgoing administration. You all know that I am a regular visitor to Nigeria; so have had first-hand experience of the impact. But as a person with social awareness and concerns for the most vulnerable in our society, here's my tuppence worth. Poverty stares you even more in the face, in today's Nigeria. There has truly been a general decline in security and quality of life – from fuel scarcity, to not having access to cash from banks and ATMs. Let's not even touch on what happened during COVID or consider the current rampant kidnapping and senseless killing of innocent people in their communities. Let me not digress.

Neither am I here to focus on the winner, or the (s) election process. I don't have enough writing space. But I have a request for the new President, Governors and other elected officials. Here it is.

Today is Children's Day and is being celebrated in Nigeria. Thanks to my Nigerian bank's marketing emails, I always know what Day it is!

As we say, 'children are our future'. Any politician that fails to consider this and the future that they are creating for the children of their country should not take the Oath of Office. Likewise, a President who cannot protect children and give them hope for a future, doesn't deserve the post.

THREE SIMPLE REQUESTS TO MR PRESIDENT

Dear Mr President, I'm not going to give you a long list of requests, but please deliver on these for now. I may add more later!

1. Make education truly free – No hidden charges for books, desks or chairs. No examination fees for WAEC or basic education qualifications. This is one of the greatest barriers to education for children from poor or low-income households. It is also one of the major causes for children dropping out of education. Don't just be blinded by unverified statistics presented to you at Cabinet meetings. Check and also work with NGOs supporting disadvantaged communities. They can tell you how it really is for poorer households living in Nigeria.

2. Enforce education laws. Child hawkers should not be on our streets in the 21st century, neither should we have young children as 'house maids' in any home or other capacity. Can't make this any clearer.

3. Prioritise projects and actions that will create opportunities for youths and young adults. It will also stem 'Japa'. Besides, our youths are not 'lazy'. They are some of the most creative people in the world today – evident in different sectors; music, film, technology, construction and many others. For goodness sake, our young people are breaking Guinness world records, effortlessly.

Deliver on these, Mr President, and see Nigeria become the Giant of Africa, again.

God bless Nigeria in our New Dawn.

- 27th May 2023

GLOSSARY OF NIGERIAN TERMINOLOGIES

Oooo!: Often used as an expression to emphasise the preceding word or sentence. May also be used as a warning e.g. 'don't try me oooo!'

Wahala: Trouble, stress, drama

Naija: Modern expression of being a Nigerian. It implies a new vibe and disassociation with the negative image often linked with the formal description 'Nigerian'.

Oyinbo: Caucasian or light skinned person. Can also be used to describe a foreigner, or a Nigerian who doesn't understand the local way of doing things i.e. haggling for lower prices at the market.

Aso-ebi: Uniform traditional fabric that is provided for all invited guests to wear to events such as weddings, birthdays and funerals. It can be styled in many ways, as the wearer chooses. Usually, will have *gele* as part of the outfit.

Gele: Traditional female head gear worn with African print materials. At times used for social occasions and styled in different ways.

Owambe: A party like no other. Loud, noisy, carnival style. A high celebration filled with colourful people and swagger. Not for introverts.

Japa: A recent term to describe the trend of Nigerians, mostly young professionals, relocating abroad for better opportunities due to economic hardship in Nigeria.

Garri: Dried cassava grains, usually eaten with African pepper stews/sauce. A staple in low-income homes. Often soaked in water as a stomach filler, when no other food is available.

Full chest: Owning what you say or do. With abandon.

Choke: becoming emotional or being shocked.

Amebo: Gossip, gist, talkative

Ejo or Biko: Please

Bawoni: General greeting in Yoruba. Hello. How are you? What's up.

ABOUT THE AUTHOR

Michelle Ronke is a Nigerian British woman who lives in Hertfordshire, UK. She is an advocate for emotional well-being and self-care.

Michelle is proud of her bicultural heritage and life experiences, which gives her a lot of interesting things to talk and write about. This is her first published book.

Printed in Great Britain
by Amazon